中国能源革命进展报告

能源技术革命

（2021）

国务院发展研究中心资源与环境政策研究所　编著

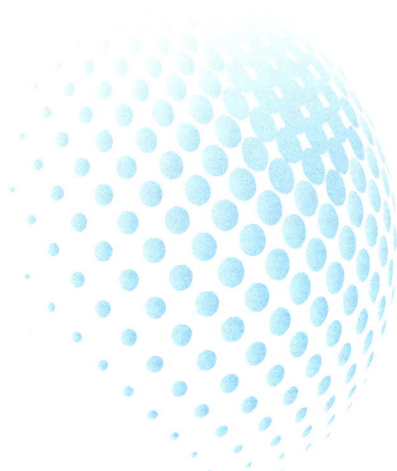

北　京

冶金工业出版社

2021

图书在版编目（CIP）数据

中国能源革命进展报告：能源技术革命.2021/国务院
发展研究中心资源与环境政策研究所编著.—北京：冶金
工业出版社，2021.9

ISBN 978-7-5024-8933-5

Ⅰ.①中… Ⅱ.①国… Ⅲ.①能源发展—研究报告—
中国—2021 Ⅳ.①F426.2

中国版本图书馆 CIP 数据核字（2021）第 187691 号

出 版 人　苏长永

地　　　址　北京市东城区嵩祝院北巷 39 号　邮编　100009　电话　（010）64027926
网　　　址　www.cnmip.com.cn　电子信箱　yjcbs@cnmip.com.cn
责任编辑　曾　媛　刘小峰　美术编辑　彭子赫　版式设计　彭子赫
责任校对　李　娜　责任印制　李玉山
ISBN 978-7-5024-8933-5
冶金工业出版社出版发行；各地新华书店经销；三河市双峰印刷装订有限公司印刷
2021 年 9 月第 1 版，2021 年 9 月第 1 次印刷
787mm×1092mm　1/16；8.25 印张；120 千字
100.00 元
冶金工业出版社　投稿电话　（010）64027932　投稿信箱　tougao@cnmip.com.cn
冶金工业出版社营销中心　电话　（010）64044283　传真　（010）64027893
冶金工业出版社天猫旗舰店　yjgycbs.tmall.com
（本书如有印装质量问题，本社营销中心负责退换）

《中国能源革命进展报告——能源技术革命（2021）》

编 委 会

前　　言

　　自 2014 年习近平主席提出推动能源消费、供给、技术和体制革命并全方位加强国际合作的能源安全新战略以来，中国深化体制改革，加强科技创新，在建设清洁低碳、安全高效的现代能源体系方面取得较大进步。能源技术创新在能源革命中起决定性作用，中国贯彻创新、协调、绿色、开放、共享的新发展理念，制定和实施了能源技术革命创新行动计划，促进能源科技发展、能源技术创新和能源产业升级，从理论到实践都取得积极进展。

　　中国能源技术革命理论进入新境界。习近平主席关于能源革命的重要论述，开辟了中国特色能源发展理论的新高度。在"十三五"时期，技术创新推动能源绿色低碳发展，全面推进构建清洁低碳、智慧高效、经济安全的新型能源体系。2021 年 5 月，习主席在中国科协第十次全国代表大会上更进一步提出，中国坚持把科技创新摆在国家发展全局的核心位置，在重要科技领域实现跨越式发展，推动关键核心技术自主可控，加强创新链产业链融合。科技攻关要坚持问题导向，奔着最紧急、最紧迫的问题去，在煤炭、油气、风电、光伏、水电、核电等方面关键核心技术上全力攻坚、加快突破。着力推动新一代信息技术与能源清洁高效开发利用技术的融合创新，大力发展智慧能源技术，把能源技术及其关联产业培育成带动产业升级的新增长点。

　　中国能源技术革命实践取得新进展。2014 年以来，"四个革命、一个合作"能源安全新战略稳步推进，中国能源技术水平和能力伴随着能源革命深入同步壮大，多项能源自主关键技术跃居国际领先水平，技术进步成为推动能源发展动力变革的基本力量。煤炭绿色高效智能开采技术取得进展，大型煤矿采煤机械化程度达 98%，掌握煤制油气产业化技术，甲醇制烯烃技术持续创新带动了中国煤制烯烃产业快速发展。油气勘探开发技术水平不断进步，页岩油气勘探开发技术和装备水平大幅提升，低渗原油及稠油高效开发、新一代复合化学驱等技术世界领先。完备的水电、风电、太阳能发电、核电等清洁能源装备制造产业链已经建立，成功研发制造全球最大单机容量100万千瓦水电机组，具备最大单机容量达10兆瓦的全系列风电机组制造能力，不断刷新光伏电池转换效率世界纪录；已建成若干应用先进三代技术的核电站，世界首座具有第四代先进核能系统特征的高温气冷堆示范工程成功临界，机组正式开启带核功率运行，小型堆等多项核能利用技术取得明显突破。已建成规模最大、安全可靠、全球领先的电网，供电可靠性位居世界前列。"互联网+"智慧能源、储能、区块链、综合能源服务等一大批能源新技术、新模式、新业态正在蓬勃兴起。当前，随着低碳技术的加速研发、日趋成熟和广泛应用，能源技术正在成为引领能源产业变革，实现碳达峰和碳中和目标的源动力。

百年未有之大变局催生世界能源技术新变革。近年来，地缘战略、大国博弈、军备竞赛等传统安全议题愈发上升为全球事务和国际关系的中心议题，叠加全球新型冠状病毒肺炎（简称"新冠肺炎"）疫情这一"超级非传统安全"难题，使得国际关系发展的不确定性因素显著增加。"后新冠肺炎时代"的世界经济增长存在较大不确定性，全球能源市场大幅波动仍将持续，国际能源格局正在出现深度调整，同时能源技术将加速变革助力疫情后全球经济绿色复苏和应对气候变化。绿色低碳正成为能源技术创新的主要方向，重点集中在传统化石能源清洁高效利用、新能源大规模开发利用、核能安全利用、能源互联网和大规模储能示范应用等领域；能源技术创新进入高度活跃期，新兴能源技术正以前所未有的速度加速迭代，对世界能源格局和经济发展将产生重大而深远的影响。

中国能源技术革命既面临重大挑战也有难得机遇。随着中美大国战略竞争博弈日趋激烈，美国在对中国打起"贸易牌、科技牌、金融牌"后，正在打出"能源牌、气候牌"。欧盟推动经济可持续发展与绿色经济复苏面临前所未有的挑战，欧、美等发达国家和地区推动实施的碳边境调节机制引起的国际经贸规则新变化必将对中国深度参与国际产业链和供应链产生深远影响。能源科技基础理论薄弱环节更为凸显，"卡脖子"技术问题更加突出，低碳技术体系建设困难重重。面对世界百年未有之大变局加速演变带给我们的艰巨挑战，中国将努力在危机中育新机、于变局中开新局。特别是运用新型举国体制提升能源创新体系整体效能，将促使创新链产业链加快融合，逐渐摆脱对国外的技术依赖，使技术创新成为实现 2030 年前二氧化碳达峰、2060 年前碳中和（简称"3060"）战略目标的强有力支撑。

技术决定能源未来、技术创造未来能源。无论是非化石能源的快速发展，还是化石能源的清洁利用，都将更多依赖跨界科技创新来驱动。中国能源领域正朝向高度数字化、低碳化方向演进，未来 5G、物联网、人工智能、区块链、云计算、大数据、边缘计算等新兴技术与能源领域的深度融合，将为实现能源革命和"3060"战略目标铺设一条数字之路。为此，国务院发展研究中心组织业内的一批资深专家学者，遵循习近平主席的一系列重要讲话和指示批示精神，针对中国能源革命战略思想发布以来，全国各部门、各地区、科研机构、高等院校、行业协会、重点企业等推动能源技术革命的实践和探索进行系统总结，立足新发展阶段，梳理能源领域低碳化转型亟待解决的科学问题和技术瓶颈，展望未来十年全球和中国能源技术革命发展方向、数字化关键技术及发展前景，以期更好地服务于中国"3060"战略目标，持续推动中国能源技术革命向纵深挺进，为中国 2030 年前二氧化碳达峰和能源行业"十四五"谋新篇、开新局提供强力支撑。

目　　录

一、"十三五"时期能源技术革命取得显著成效

"十三五"时期，中国深入实施创新驱动发展战略，构建绿色、低碳、智慧能源技术创新体系，着力提升能源科技和装备水平。大力推动能源技术与新一代信息技术和先进制造技术等深度融合，依托"互联网+"智慧能源建设，探索能源生产和消费方式创新新路子。加快风电、光伏等领域的新型可再生能源技术创新，支持中国可再生能源从产业先进向技术领先迈进；数字光伏创新升级，推动光伏发电与农业、渔业、建筑等技术融合发展，拓展光伏发电互补应用新空间；加速发展绿氢制取、储运和应用等氢能产业链技术装备，有力促进氢燃料电池汽车产业链发展；支持能源各环节各场景储能技术和装备研发及应用，着力推进储能与可再生能源互补发展；在试点示范项目和工程引领和带动下，各类能源新技术、新模式、新业态持续涌现，形成能源创新发展的"乘数效应"，为2030年前实现二氧化碳达峰奠定良好技术基础。

（一）化石能源领域技术

"十三五"时期，化石能源领域以助力构建清洁低碳、智慧高效、经济安全的能源体系为目标，立足发展阶段需要，顺应全球技术发展趋势，推进数字化升级，攻克部分制约行业发展的关键技术难题，形成了一批具有国际先进水平的技术，为保障煤炭和油气供应安全提供了有力支撑。

1. 煤炭

"十三五"时期，煤炭行业自主创新能力得到大幅提升，建立起以企业为主体、以市场为导向、产学研协同创新的科技创新体系，初步形成功能互补、导向明确的行业研发平台和创新基地合理布局，煤炭科技实

现了从跟踪、模仿到部分领域并跑、领跑的转变。目前已初步形成以煤矿安全高效生产为重点的煤矿地质保障体系，井下槽波地震、无线电波透视探测技术、定向长钻孔钻进、碎软煤层气体定向钻进技术与装备已达到国际领先水平，三维地震勘探、直流电法、瞬变电磁、地质雷达等技术已得到广泛应用。建立了安全、高效、绿色开采技术体系，开发了掘锚机组、自移式机尾、运锚机等快掘系统，形成了固体充填、膏体充填、高水材料充填等多种减沉技术，开展了8.8米超大采高工作面开采，提出了"无人操作、有人巡视"的智能化开采生产模式。完善了涵盖煤炭加工、利用、转化与污染物控制的洁净煤技术体系。测算结果显示，先进产能煤矿煤炭开采环节，吨煤碳排放量低于非先进产能煤矿50%以上，有效地降低了碳排放强度。

一是地质勘探领域，建成与中国煤炭资源分布特点相适应的煤炭资源综合勘查技术体系，将"煤田地质勘探"发展为以煤为主、包含煤层气、页岩气、致密砂岩气等多能源矿产协同勘查，并涵盖煤炭勘查、矿井建设、安全生产、环境保护等内容的"煤炭资源综合勘查"。成功研发了矿井灾害源超深探测地质雷达装备和技术方法，探测距离可达80米、距离提高1.6倍以上，地质构造验证率平均达75%；开发了矿井低频地质雷达探测系统及计算机层析成像（CT）透视反演软件，实现透射法300米跨度工作面探测、精度提高30%以上。二是煤炭开发领域，煤机装备制造水平位于世界先列，研制成功8.8米一次采全高、7.0米超大采高智能综放、纯水液压支架等系列成套装备。全国已建成500个左右智能化采掘工作面，采煤工作面机器人群、钻锚机器人、选矸机器人和巡检机器人已在煤矿井下应用，形成了薄煤层和中厚煤层智能化无人操作、大采高煤层人–机–环智能耦合高效综采、综放工作面智能化操控与人工干预辅助放煤、复杂条件智能化+机械化等4种智能化开采模式。煤矿智能化建设持续推进煤炭生产方式变革，推动各生产环节的智能化联动，有效减少井下作业人数。2020年底山西省力推煤矿智能化建设，有望实现智能化采煤工作面减人达60%–70%、智能化煤矿减人达50%以上。三是煤化工领域，在煤制烯烃、煤制乙二醇等技术和装备方面均取得了较大突破，其中生产工艺、关键大型装备和特殊催化剂等方面逐步实现了国产化。已完成煤制油品/烯烃大型现代煤化工成套技术开发与应用，首创了高效大型现代煤制油品和烯烃工程化技术，世界首个煤直接液化和煤制烯烃工程实现长周期稳定运行。

（1）地质勘探

数字煤炭地质遥感技术。基于高分遥感数据的人工智能（AI）监测系统，融合大体量数据传输和处理技术，快速提取空间规划目标图斑，集成遥感技术数字探测、监测与应用，确定地表和地下煤系或煤层的空间位置，圈定其空间边界。数字化地质遥感技术具有视域广、智能快速、透视性强等功能。重点突破了遥感地质解译中的反演问题，通过机器识别进行参数调控，剔除影响干扰反演质量因素，得到精度更高、效果更好的地质解释结果。初步解决了地震、测井数据体量大和多源异构等造成的煤炭资源评价难等问题。目前已形成了航空高光谱、航天高分辨率、地面探测，以及全球定位系统（GPS）、地理信息系统（GIS）、遥感（RS）相结合的较为完善的"3S"技术应用研究体系，广泛应用于干旱、半干旱区域大规模快速扫面工作，为煤炭区域探测、开采动态监测、采后采空区圈定提供依据。

数字化航空电磁法探测技术。采用对象驱动取代数据驱动，融合快速无线通信技术、智能识别、提取靶体信息技术和海量数据非线性反演技术等，将地质信息利用机器学习方法进行场值标定，通过并行集群进行三维反演形成三维地质解释。具有运行速度快、适应环境能力强、数据采集量大等特点，初步形成了固定翼、吊舱式电磁法相结合，地-空电磁法辅助的探测体系。基本解决了基于对象驱动噪声压制关键问题，得到具有更高信噪比、更深地质信息的信号，提高了煤炭资源探测水平，广泛应用于丘陵、高原等地形地质复杂地区基础地质、能源勘查与评价等方面。

（2）煤炭开采

数字化快速掘进技术。基于掘锚支运一体化空间多维度同步技术，将掘进工程进行系统一体化设计，通过掘进工艺和装备创新构建各工序同步作业线，大幅提高成巷效率。基本攻克了掘支平行、全宽截割、自动支护、柔性运输、协同控制、智能安防等核心技术难题，实现各设备自动测距跟进、连续运输、煤流均衡、协同运动控制等功能。目前研制的模块化智能锚杆转载机、柔性连续运输系统等成套设备及平台，成功应用于地质覆存条件好的大型煤矿区，增加了设备运行效率，提升了设备安全智能化水平，实现了协同控制系统自调试性、自组织性和自稳定性。

智能化开采技术。基于在自动化系统中加入自主决策功能，使其能够实时感知围岩条件及外部环境的变化并自动调整开采参数，具有智能感知、智能决策和智能控制三大功能，实现自主学习和自主决策，可做到自适应开采。黄陵一号煤矿1.4-2.2米较薄中厚煤层智能化改造后，可做到工作面常态化一人巡视、地面调度中心或巷道集控中心监控的智能化开采，实现了煤炭无人开采技术的新突破。攻克了8.2米厚煤层一次采全高技术难题，在国内外首次研发了8.2米综采成套技术和智能化控制系统，并在金鸡滩煤矿成功应用，创出月产原煤202万吨的纪录，达到国际领先水平。

（3）清洁转化

燃煤发电技术。主要包括以锅炉为核心的燃烧技术，以及各类泵、给水加热器、凝汽器、管道、水冷壁等汽水技术，汽轮发电机、主变压器等电气技术和控制技术等。将煤炭的化学能转化为电能，主要装备包括亚临界燃煤发电机组、超临界燃煤发电机组和超超临界燃煤发电机组等。"十三五"时期中国燃煤发电技术水平位居世界前列，并不断向高参数、大容量、高效及低排放方向发展。燃煤发电技术的清洁转化主要采用四类技术以提高效率和降低排放：一是通过用大容量高参数的先进燃煤发电机组替代落后高能耗的小机组，其中以超临界和超超临界技术为代表；二是利用煤化工中已成熟的煤气化技术，集成蒸汽燃气联合循环技术实现清洁高效发电，其中以整体煤气化联合循环发电技术（IGCC）为代表；三是利用生物质燃料与煤炭进行掺烧，用生物质替代部分燃煤与煤电耦合发电，减少耗煤量和排放量，以生物质气化与煤混燃耦合发电技术为代表；四是现役机组的节能改造、超低排放改造、灵活性改造、优化运行等，以数字煤电厂技术为代表。超超临界发电技术具备可靠、大型、高效、清洁等特点，基本解决了燃煤发电效率提高和节能减排等问题。中国 60 万千瓦超超临界燃煤机组供电煤耗 278 克/千瓦时，比同容量亚临界机组的煤耗少 30 克/千瓦时，每年可比同容量亚临界机组节约 6 万吨标准煤。IGCC 技术具有发电效率高、环保性能好的特点，但因系统复杂导致投资偏高。生物质与燃煤耦合发电技术综合利用多种能源，可初步解决传统能源短缺、生物质资源露天堆积、焚烧浪费、减污降碳等问题。随着煤电技术与信息通信技术逐渐融合，数字煤电厂改造技术路线日益成熟、经济成本日趋合理、改造效果日渐明显。数字煤电厂以智能管理及三维技术等数字化设计方法建设管理，具有三维建模、大数据平台、机器人巡检等功能，基本解决了提高火电厂发电能效、提高生产运行安全、降低设备运维成本、提升火电机组调峰能力、降低环境污染物及碳排放等科学问题。截至 2020 年，全国有 8.9 亿千瓦煤电机组达到超低排放水平，占煤电总装机容量 10.8 亿千瓦的 80% 以上，建成了全球最大的清洁煤电供应体系。

煤制油品/烯烃煤化工技术。攻克了煤直接液化和煤制烯烃工程放大、关键装备与超大超厚设备制造、系统集成的稳定性和可靠性、装置安全稳定长周期运行等系列世界性难题，形成具有自主知识产权的百万吨级煤直接液化和 60 万吨级煤制烯烃成套技术，并建成世界首个示范工程，以及世界上单厂生产能力最大的 400 万吨/年煤间接液化产业化示范项目。建造了具有自主知识产权的"神宁炉"，其合成柴油具有超低硫（接近零）、低芳烃、低灰分、高十六烷值的特点，而且二氧化硫、氮氧化物、烟尘烟气排放指标远远低于国家标准。

2. 石油天然气

"十三五"时期，油气行业面对国际油价大幅波动的挑战，加快转变发展方式，实施了保障化、差异化、低成本、国际化和一体化等发展战略，着力推动高质量发展，突出发展质量和效益，加强改革和创新，发挥新型举国体制机制优势进行攻关，在深部油气勘探开发、非常规油气勘探开发、炼化智能一体化管控、智能油品销售等领域的关键技术或技术应用开发达到国际先进水平，有力地支撑油气行业绿色、高效发展。2020年，国内原油产量达到1.95亿吨、天然气产量约1900亿立方米，行业能耗增速由"十二五"时期的6.9%降至2020年的3%，二氧化碳排放量在油气勘探开发领域约1亿吨、炼化领域约5亿吨。

一是勘探开发领域，形成了东部断陷盆地精细勘探理论和评价、海相深层碳酸盐岩油气成藏理论和评价、中西部致密碎屑岩油气差异富集规律和甜点评价、海相页岩气富集机理的理论和勘探评价、陆相页岩油气赋存机理与分类评价、被动大陆边缘盆地油气成藏理论和深水勘探评价、单点高密度地震与高端成像软件平台、特深层勘探工程等勘探关键技术，开发了特深层油气开发工程、常压和深层页岩气低成本开发技术、非均相复合驱、高含硫气田提高采收率、致密油气有效开发、特深层钻完井等开发关键技术，研制了旋转导向仪器、高温高压定向测井仪、高性能自动化智能化钻机及压裂车、新型高效破岩工具等特种作业装备，推进了勘探开发技术和装备数字化升级，基本实现了不同类型油气藏高质量勘探和效益开发。二是炼油化工领域，已掌握了世界先进水平的炼油全流程技术，涵盖从重油深度催化裂解制取低碳烯烃、多产异构烷烃催化劣化工艺、S-Zorb汽油吸附脱硫、低压连续重整、催化柴油转化生产高辛烷值汽油技术，到柴油超深度加氢脱硫、柴油液相循环加氢等技术；拥有了具有自主知识产权的石油化工主体技术，包括百万吨级乙烯成套技术、CBL-IX型重质原料裂解炉、大型芳烃配套技术、连续重整技术、丙烯烷基化制异丙苯成套技术、双氧水法丙烯制环氧丙烷成套技术、新一代高性能苯乙烯类热塑性弹性体技术、环己酮氨肟化制己内酰胺技术、甲苯甲醇甲基化制二甲苯技术等；实现了裂解气压缩机、环氧乙烷反应器、聚酯主反应器、加氢裂化反应器、渣油加氢反应器、百万吨级压缩机组等重大装备的国产化；突破了一批化工新材料关键技术，包括碳纤维及其复合材料制造、特高分子量高密度聚乙烯锂电池隔膜、超高压聚乙烯电缆专用料、聚丙烯输液袋专用料、化纤生物降解材料、氢化苯乙烯热塑性弹性体、阻燃腈纶纤维等。三是油气储运领域，大力发展管道运输、推进油库布局调整，形成了调运灵活、吞吐自如、存销平衡、保障供给的成品油储运网络，建成了西南、甬台温、绍兴-杭州、湛江等多条成品油销售管道和北京长辛店等多座成品油油库。四是油品销售领域，构建了以自有分销通路为基础的网络化经营体系，逐渐打破地域限制，基本形成全国性成品油销售网络。已初步开发完成具有成品油销售特色的大型分布式多层架构加油站管理信息系统并开始应用，成功建成了全球最大的成品油销售管理信息技术群，创新了具有鲜明中国特色的加油机、计量计价、加油卡、加油站前庭等技术，逐步引入互联网支付、营销等手段以满足日益增长的消费者新需求，并在大型企业推广应用，有效支撑大型成品油销售网络的标准化、集约化发展。

（1）勘探开发

数字化油气勘探技术。基于地质、物探（包括地震勘探与重、磁、电、化探等）、地球物理测井等手段，利用三维可视化、大数据管理平台等新一代信息技术集成了信息化勘探技术体系。助力解决了因勘探技术获取的数字内容资源多源、异构、体量大等特点造成的油气资源评价、储层预测和岩性识别难等问题，以满足储层评价及识别、参数预测等方面的数字化需求，实现精准、高效的储层预测、油藏评价与描述。

数字化油气开发技术。以渗流力学理论为基础，结合油层物理实际情况，分析储集层和流体渗流规律，构建数字油气藏，在虚拟环境中实现真实油藏的动态模拟及生产环境的感知、分析、预测、优化和决策。初步解决了生产方案决策、产量预测模型、工作流程模拟，以及油气地面工程建设和采油工程一体化等存在的问题，可基本满足油气开发实时调控、生产措施优选、站场设备安全和数字化计量及安全运行等方面的需求。

数字化油气成井技术。基于自动化钻机、井下高精度测量仪器、可视化设备、精细钻完井设计等，通过近钻头实时数据传输，利用数字化平台、远程决策支持中心等形成了信息化钻完井技术体系。初步解决了复杂地层井眼靶点定向、轨迹优化、提速提效难等问题，可初步满足井下精准测量控制、复杂状况与事故及时准确预测、钻井参数动态优化、装备在线预警与诊断等方面的工程需求。

（2）炼油化工

数字化生产管控一体化技术。利用炼化生产装置的数据采集、流程控制和生产优化分析等技术，通过对工艺流程、生产管理及产品营销等过程进行数字建模、仿真与优化，初步形成虚拟与现实结合的数字化工厂的技术体系。基本解决了生产原料、工艺流程及生产管控复杂，以及产品种类多、受市场价格影响大等导致的炼化生产过程控制难度高等问题，可满足炼厂原油（料）与能源供应协同运行，以及产品储运和市场营销服务、生产管理的全业务链数字一体化建设需求。

数字化设备安全监测与控制技术。利用数字化监测控制、设备实时态势预测、数字化风险管理等技术，可实现设备状态辨识与预测、外部环境扰动或自身故障自适应调节控制和自主式维修保障决策。初步解决了炼厂全生命周期生产过程中设备可靠性、稳定性的问题，可满足炼厂生产运行安全可靠和人、机、环境和谐共处的需求。

（3）油品销售

线上交易平台技术。利用互联网端的新技术与新理念，通过建设业务服务中心及对数据的综合存储利用，贯通寻源、议价、销售、配送各环节业务，形成了可实现成品油线上下单、商品管理、价格管理、促销管理、物流跟踪、客户评价等线上全流程交易技术。初步解决了客户快捷连接、油品快速销售、结算准确快速等难点问题，可提升"以客户为中心"的成品油销售企业互联网端的服务能力。

数字加油站技术。基于智能卡、数据仓库等技术，构建覆盖成品油进、销、存、量、价的零售管理系统的技术体系。基本解决了大型石油公司加油站点多、线长、面广的多层级管理问题，可实现对加油站网络生产经营数据的准确采集、及时掌握，做到对车队客户加油及资金的安全管理服务，满足成品油销售公司内部管理和经营风险防控需要。

（4）天然气发电

天然气发电技术包括燃气轮机、汽轮机、发电机、换热器和泵等技术，主要设备包括燃气-蒸汽联合循环机组和天然气分布式多联供机组等。目前中国的燃气-蒸汽联合循环机组多采用 9E、9F 级等大型燃气轮机，在发电效率、启动时间、排放量和灵活性方面均有改善。天然气分布式多联供技术，通过燃气轮机、燃气内燃机、微燃机等热动力机组发电，再将产生的高温烟气、冷却水等通过余热利用机组生产冷、热，满足电、热、冷等终端能源需求。天然气发电各类污染物排放和碳排放量相较于煤电具有显著优势，9HA 燃机电厂度电二氧化碳排放量（313 克）较煤电厂排放低一半以上，度电的氮氧化物排放量（0.07 克）比 660 兆瓦燃煤电厂低 0.1 克左右，硫化物和烟尘排放均接近于零。

（二）非化石能源领域技术

截至 2020 年，中国非化石能源发电装机 9.5 亿千瓦，占全国发电装机的 43%，其中风电 2.8 亿千瓦、光伏发电 2.5 亿千瓦、水电 3.7 亿千瓦、核电 0.5 亿千瓦[①]。非化石能源发电技术快速发展，装备制造产业链已经建立，在非化石能源装机、发电量保持较高增速的同时，弃电量和弃电率均降低，较 2015 年分别提高 10% 左右，实现"双升双降"。通过能源结构优化和能效提升，单位发电量二氧化碳排放强度比 2015 年降低 10% 左右。

1. 风能

风力发电技术是利用风机的叶片和传动系统将风能转化为机械能，再通过发电机将机械能转化为电能的发电技术。中国从 2005 年开始大规模发展风电，到 2010 年风电累计装机规模成为全球第一并保持至今，年新增装机保持在千万千瓦级的规模；中国风电装备制造产业也实现了技术上的跟跑甚至领跑。风力发电技术根据应用场景可分为陆上集中式风电、陆上分散式风电及海上风电等。

陆上风电技术。涵盖风轮直径达到 156 米、风机机型为 4-8 兆瓦乃

---

① 数据来源：2020 年全国电力工业统计快报一览表。

至 10 兆瓦及以上、风速最低可下探至 4.5 米/秒的风电机组整机设计、研发和建造技术，以及叶片、齿轮箱、发电机、电控系统等一系列技术体系。中国陆上风电技术和装备水平达到国际一流，风电机组技术呈现大型化、智能化、高效化、高可靠性的发展趋势。风机功率不断提高，目前国内吊装陆上风电最大单机容量为 10 兆瓦；风机发电量较 10 年前相同容量的风机发电量增长 2 倍以上；低风速、高塔筒技术不断创新，大幅提升了陆上风能资源的经济可开发量。

分散式风电技术。分散式风电具有规模小、接入电压等级低、可就近接入当地电网进行消纳的特点，针对土地资源紧缺、距离居民近等特点，形成了基础深埋技术、防腐蚀技术、降噪技术等适应性强的一系列技术体系。可应用于工业园区、田间地埂、人工渔礁等场景。

海上风电技术。涵盖风机机型为 6 兆瓦至 14 兆瓦及以上、单桩基础、导管架基础、抗冰能力、柔性直流传输和深远海大型汇流站设计及研发等一系列技术体系。中国海上风机基础设计能力不断提高，运输安装施工技术取得长足进步，主要零部件制造和关键技术取得突破，与国际先进水平齐平。

数字风电技术。以大数据和互联网为基础，以风电的激光雷达等新型传感技术、增强气动技术、风功率预测、故障预测、寿命分析等系统技术为依托，形成了智能风电场设计、精确选址、风机选型、智能控制、风电场运行优化和调度支持系统等一系列技术体系。通过对风电场和风电机组的智能化升级，可有效提高风电机组出力、降低风电场和风机的故障率和运维成本，降低风电的度电成本。

2. 太阳能

光伏发电技术。基于太阳能电池方阵、蓄电池组、充放电控制器、逆变器、交流配电柜、太阳跟踪控制系统等设备和技术形成技术体系。目前产业化技术处于世界先进水平，前沿技术加速布局，主要装备制造均已实现国产化。中国新增光伏装机规模从 2013 年起、累计装机规模从 2015 年起、产业规模从 2007 年起已连续多年位居世界第一。2020 年，中国共 4 次创造了世界太阳能电池最高效率的纪录，新增光伏市场中主流光伏组件平均转化效率达到 20% 以上。

太阳能热发电技术。利用大规模阵列抛物或碟形镜面收集太阳热能，通过换热装置提供蒸汽，结合传统汽轮发电机的工艺实现发电，目前主要包括塔式、槽式、碟式和菲涅尔式四类技术。国内太阳能热发电设备制造企业产品涵盖了太阳能聚光部件、吸热部件、传热储热及材料、汽轮发电机组、集成控制系统、辅助系统等 6 大类，基本覆盖了太阳能热发电建设的全产业链。截至 2020 年，全国太阳能热发电累计装机约 45 万千瓦。

数字光伏电站技术。涵盖光伏系统规划、建设、运行等各环节的数字化技术和预测、运行控制及运维技术等组成的技术体系，具有运行监测数据实时采集、远程监控、远程自动运维、自动清洗、故障远程诊断和快速处理等特征。基本解决了光伏电站最小单元的精细化管理，提升光伏系统发电效率、实时感知光伏出力波动性、安全稳定和智能运维等问题，实现人力成本节省的同时可增强电站运维的预警能力和抗风险能力。可应用于集中式光伏电站、楼宇建筑光伏、路面光伏、光伏廊道和光伏景观等，从定期检修到状态检修，从被动巡检到主动巡检，实现远程少人运维，做到"无人值班，少人值守"。

3. 水能

中国水电结构优化加快推进，外送通道建设大规模开展，技术装备水平稳步提升，全产业链"出海"步伐加快。"十三五"时期，核准开工大型常规水电工程约 3000 万千瓦，随着金沙江白鹤滩等大型水电水利工程开工，中国黄河上游、乌江、红水河、雅砻江、大渡河、金沙江等大型水电基地开发布局已基本完成，装机容量 25 兆瓦及以下的小型水电技术逐渐退出。

大型水力发电技术。涵盖水利资源评估技术、水力发电开发技术、水工建筑物工程技术、水电站设备设计安装与运维技术、水电站运行技术等一系列技术体系，将水的重力势能和动能转变成机械能、水轮机带动发电机旋转，最终将机械能转变成电能。"十三五"时期，中国在全球最大单机容量 100 万千瓦水电机组研制成功并正式投产，在 300 米级别高坝设计、超大型地下厂房设计、复杂输水系统过渡过程分析、巨型输水系统结构设计等大型水电关键技术和相关科学问题上取得突破，从"跟跑者"逐步到"并行者"，现已成为"领跑者"。

智能水电站技术。基于智能传感器获取运行状态数据，利用新一代信息技术，形成具有信息化和数字仿真计算、在线建设管理、在线控制预警等特征的技术体系，可监控生产现场，预报与诊断事故，提供实时电机状况信息，实现水电站建设、运行、管理、调控的一体化，做到多个水电站的集中运维和集中监控，提升大坝安全化、少人化和无人化水平。基本解决了水电工程建设中的地质环境、结构形态、管理程序、进度计划的实时动态分析和耦合仿真预测问题，可确保大坝安全、及时正确采集数据制定发电计划、提高发电可控性、减少人力和人工干预、降低运营成本。

4. 核能

核能发电技术是核能在民用领域最具代表性的应用。经过三十余年的努力，中国从无到有，从弱到强，现已掌握最先进的第四代核电设计、制造和运维技术，率先实现第四代核电技术落地，此外，新一代核电技术、小型堆等多项核能利用技术也取得明显突破。截至 2020 年，核电在运装机规模约 5000 万千瓦，装机容量约 1000 万千瓦。

先进三代及四代核电技术。中国自主研发了百万千瓦级三代核电"华龙一号"和"国和一号"，主要技术和安全性能指标均处世界先进水平。该型号的技术特点主要是反应堆具有更高的可用性和更长的使用寿命、更低的严重事故概率和堆芯损伤频率，采用能动加非能动安全技术，使发生事故 72 小时内不用干预，进一步提升了核电安全性。目前，中国核电已形成了较完备的产业体系，自主成套能力达到 8-10 套/年左右，主泵、压力容器、堆内构件、燃料元件、蒸汽发生器、数字化仪控系统（DCS）、超大型铸锻件等重大装备和关键材料实现国产化，国产化率达到 85% 以上。2021 年 9 月，中国第四代核电技术高温气冷堆建设取得突破，石岛湾高温气冷堆核电站示范工程逐步趋近并首次达到临界，机组正式进入"持续核反应"状态。全球首座模块式高温气冷堆核电站，示范工程设备制造国产化率达到 93.4%，标志着中国在世界先进核能技术领域完成了从"跟跑"到"领跑"的飞跃。

小型化核反应堆技术。由于应用目的差异，小型化反应堆种类繁多，以"玲龙一号"为代表的小型化核反应堆技术已取得了突破性进展，单台输出功率在 30 万千瓦以下，具有小型化、模块化、一体化等技术特征。安全性高、灵活性好、用途广泛，可直接作为分布式电源设置在工业区和人口密集区，实现城市区域供电、供热和工业工艺供热，或海洋资源开发及海水淡化。

数字反应堆技术。基于反应堆基础理论、数值计算技术、计算机技术发展到一定阶段的综合性技术，也称为虚拟反应堆或数值反应堆。在超大规模高性能计算系统内，利用计算软件和各种数据库，集成数值仿真模拟反应堆全寿命周期各种特性；通过高精度设计分析程序研发、分析方法的改进等措施，可实现精确分析反应堆堆芯及系统的瞬态响应特性，更精准地认知临界热流密度、包壳峰值温度等主要安全与热工限制性参数的保守裕量，支撑反应堆额定功率等总体性能参数提升。数字反应堆可提升核电厂功率、提高燃耗率、延长寿命、增加核电厂经济性。

（三）能源基础设施与需求侧节能减碳技术

"十三五"时期，中国在能源安全新战略指引下，贯彻节约资源和保护环境的基本国策，以减污降碳为重要抓手，加速能源储运调峰体系建设和数字化升级，加强节能降碳科技攻关和示范应用，持续推广先进高效节能产品设备，有力促进能源利用效率提升。

1. 能源基础设施

（1）油气储运技术

油气储运技术通过新一代感知、通信和自动控制等技术与油气管网输送、地下地上储存、天然气液化和天然气压缩等多种储运形式及技术深度融合，形成以油气储运为核心的多种能源储运数字化技术体系。着力解决全方位感知、综合性预判、自适应优化、一体化管控的油气储运系统数字化和智能化等难题，满足精细化管道运输、数字化储罐、储库运营及安全监测的信息技术需求。

数字化管网技术。通过管道工程数字化技术、管道数据采集和共享应用，利用关键管网设备的感知能力获取实时数据、构建机理模型库、预测管网运行趋势，形成数字化管网技术体系。辅助提升管网运行能力和可靠性，实现管网的可视化监控、网络化输送和智能化管理，保障油气管网的安全高效运行。满足从感知、管控、决策三方面对油气管网的安全输送和经营管理数字化提升和智能化建设需求。

数字化储存技术。基于油气储存系统具有固定厂址、与不同的输送系统关联（管道、铁路、海运及公路）、需要适应其介质的不同储存形态的特点，通过储油气站库三维设计、感应系统等，构建具备运营优化、风险管控及实时决策能力的数字油气储存管理及运营技术体系。初步解决了油气存储过程中业务监控、智能巡检、计量管理、设备安全等方面存在的信息化问题，可满足油品库存优化、储站/库安全运营、智能维护及调峰等需求，基本实现各类储库生产运行的持续优化、效益效能及安全保障最大化。

数字化液化天然气储运技术。通过实时感知生产数据，收集终端消费数据，结合可再生能源的间歇和波动特征及天然气市场价格等因素，形成液化天然气储运系统运销的数字化管控和智能化决策技术体系。初步解决了数字化运营、安全生产、智能卸船、智能气化、智能调峰等过程中存在的问题，力争实现液化天然气生产储运系统效益最大化。

（2）电网技术

截至 2020 年，220 千伏及以上输电线路回路长度 79.4 万千米，220 千伏及以上变电设备容量 45.3 亿千伏安；大量风、光、水等清洁能源从中国西部通过特高压送至东部负荷中心，中国电网发展成为世界上接入新能源规模最大、最复杂的电网[①]。大容量同塔多回技术和碳纤维复合导

---

① 资料来源：中电联《中国电力行业年度发展报告 2021》，2020 年数据来自中电联 2020 年度统计数据。

线等线路技术、1000 千伏特高压交流和±1100 千伏特高压直流技术及成套设备达到国际领先水平；多端柔性直流配电网关键技术取得重大突破，微电网技术开始试点应用；电网信息安全技术有长足进展，态势感知电网调度等技术不断创新。智能电网将现代先进的计算机、通讯、网络、传感、控制技术等应用于电力系统，具有安全、可靠、绿色、高效的特点，提高了电网安全运行、供电可靠性、用户供电质量、电网设备效率及可再生能源利用效率。

智能输电技术。主要包括输电系统的动态检测和监测技术，具有铁塔及线路运行状态实时感知、AI 技术场景识别和无人机巡检等功能特征，大幅提高设备利用率、输电安全性、输电选址选线通道规划效率，极大降低运检人身伤亡率和劳动强度，明显提升线路抵御冰灾、火灾、台风等自然灾害的能力和故障恢复速度。输电设备在线监测技术应用于架空线路故障精确定位，监测视频图像、微气象和山火，分布式光纤测温等环节；利用直升机、无人机等技术开展线路巡检，实现输电设备智能运维，以防止安全事故发生及快速定位处理故障。

智能变电技术。以全站数字化、通信平台化、信息共享标准化为基本要求，基于先进、可靠、集成、低碳的智能设备，形成具有自动信息采集、量测、控制、保护和监测等功能的技术体系。可支持电网实时自动控制、智能调节、在线分析决策、协同互动等高级功能，实现与相邻变电站、电网调度等互动，实现设备智能化、模块化、集成化和状态信息可视化，基本解决了常规变电站设备通讯介质不统一、通讯协议不统一、通讯规约局限性等问题，推进一二次融合，实时检测变电站运行状态，降低维护难度，提高运行可靠性。

智能配电技术。通过配电自动化、智能配电房、智能台区等建设，形成分布式馈线自动化覆盖、光纤覆盖、一二次融合等技术体系，具有灵活可靠、可观可控、开放兼容等基本特征。初步实现了配电系统在正常运行及事故情况下的监测、保护、控制、管理的智能化，提高了电能的可靠性和质量。

智能微电网技术。利用计算机优化控制系统、发电机优化控制系统和微网信息采集系统等，初步形成分布式电源、储能、能量转换、负荷和监控、安全保护和变流器控制等技术体系，具有微型灵活、清洁高效、自发自用、余电上网和信息优化的特点。可解决电力供应的自平衡、减少大规模分布式电源接入电网时带来的冲击、确保智能微电网系统孤岛稳定运行，以及快速并网等问题，适用于分布式电源可就地就近接入地区、工业园区、偏远地区和海岛等。

（3）储能技术

储能技术主要用于削峰填谷、平抑电能波动性、减少弃风弃光，储存的能量可用作应急能源，初步解决了能源系统的波动性和随机性问题。"十三五"时期，储电、储冷/热等技术在中国逐步得到大规模推广应用，其中抽水蓄能技术得到最为广泛的应用。

储冷/热技术。通过装置或介质将冷、热能量储存，形成实现冷、热能量的储存、释放或快速功率交换等技术体系。具有系统能量调节灵活、供冷热能可靠性高等特点，可解决综合能源系统中因时间、空间或强度上的冷热能量供给与需求间不匹配问题，提升供冷热能质量和出力特性，促进综合能源系统安全稳定运行，可应用于有电力、热力调峰需求的用户、能源站等场景。

电化学储能技术。电化学储能技术可分为铅酸电池、锂离子电池、钠硫和钒液流电池等。锂离子电池装机规模占中国电化学储能市场的88.8%，在光储充一体化充电站、分布式微网、调频辅助服务、户用储能等领域的应用快速增长。锂离子电池以三元锂、磷酸铁锂等技术为主，具有能量密度大、响应速度快、循环寿命长、转化效率高等特点；可模块化建设，受地理条件限制小，适用于移动设备、电动汽车、可再生能源并网等场景。

抽水蓄能技术。抽水蓄能电站在负荷低谷时用电将水抽至上水库，在负荷高峰期再放水至下水库发电，具有高水头、大容量、长寿命、技术成熟、经济可靠的特点。抽水蓄能电站可解决电力系统大功率调峰和电能长时间存储问题，有助于提升大规模可再生能源接入能力，减少可再生能源并网运行对电网的冲击，基本可实现电力系统的高效灵活、安全稳定运行。

2. 需求侧节能减碳技术

（1）工业领域积极推动重点行业节能技术进步

中国一直高度重视钢铁、有色、建材、石化、造纸等高耗能行业的节能减排技术进步，并取得了显著成效。其中大中型钢铁企业的可比能耗已达到日韩的先进水平，也接近德国的水平；电解铝平均电耗仅比国际先进水平高5%。不过仍有部分高耗能产品的能耗明显偏高，其中水泥平均能耗比日本先进水平高19%，造纸能耗比国际先进水平高90%。

钢铁、有色等冶金领域积极采用各种余热余压回收利用技术，实现废气、废水、废料的循环利用，不仅促进节能减排，还可降低生产成本，提高产品毛利率。同时，利用新一代信息技术改进传统生产工艺，提高冶金工艺效率，实现降耗、减排、提质。建材领域积极推进绿色制造，如水泥生产中推进先进粉磨技术，提高工艺能效；推进钢渣、矿渣粉磨技术，替代传统石灰石，实现废料循环利用；引入新型水泥熟料冷却技术及装备，提高热回收效率、输送运转率，进一步降低电耗。石化领域引进新型催化、分离和化工过程强化等关键共性技术，整体技术水平显著提高；采用新型催化材料与技术、先进的分离材料与技术，改善石化生产工艺，基本实现流程简化，降低能耗、减少污染排放。造纸领域积极推广余热回收、碱回收及中浓制浆等节能减碳技术，其中余热回收利用技术包括热泵干燥、预热机械浆的热能回收、间歇蒸煮喷放热能回收、纸机干燥部废气热回收、烟道气热回收等技术，可提高工艺能效。

（2）建筑领域在完善建筑结构和改进用能技术上多措并举

建筑领域着重考虑终端节能技术的应用。对于新建建筑，开展和投资绿色建筑、一体化建筑和被动式节能设计，推广节能绿色建材、装配式和钢结构建筑；对于存量建筑则加强节能改造，提高建筑用能系统和设备效率。国内老旧小区改造广泛采用强化围护结构和建筑保温、气密性保障等技术手段提升建筑本体的节能潜力；同时建立能效标识制度，引导采购高效智能家电、制冷、照明、办公终端等，主动降低建筑运行能耗。

清洁能源供冷热技术，泛指利用太阳能、地热能、生物质能、天然气等清洁能源满足终端用冷、用热需求的技术体系，在建筑领域得到大力推广。具有低碳环保、高效节能等特点，可根据本地能源资源禀赋，将热泵、燃气供热等多种供冷热模式进行优势互补、综合利用；可与先进的信息与通信技术结合，解决供冷热与电网、热网协同互动的问题，提升电网对可再生能源的消纳能力，降低环境污染物排放，适用于建筑、居民等有供冷热需求的场景。地热能技术主要包括了用于精细刻画地下三维空间地质结构的三维地震勘查技术，保障地热水资源采灌均衡的砂岩孔隙热储回灌、非原水回灌技术；为进一步加强地热资源监测与评价，自动数据采集与传输、大数据等新一代信息技术也被广泛应用于地热资源的开发与利用。生物质能技术主要包含高温干式和中高温半干式厌氧发酵技术，高效厌氧发酵技术，生物质成型燃料机械制造、专用锅炉制造、燃料燃烧技术等。近年来随着清洁取暖行动深入推进，包括空气源热泵、水源热泵、地源热泵等热泵技术得到广泛应用。与传统供热方式相比，热泵可集成生物质供热、蒸汽制冷、光热等，为区域能源供应提供高效率、清洁化供冷热解决方案。

（3）交通领域以电气化为主方向推动节能提效

交通领域大力发展电动车、高铁、港口岸电技术。以电能替代传统燃油装置，实现交通领域显著节能减排。积极推进制动能量回馈系统、船舶推进系统、数字化岸电系统，以及基于先进信息技术的交通运输系统等先进节能技术创新，不断改进能效。

传统燃油汽车的燃油经济性不断提升，截至 2020 年传统乘用车的百公里油耗已降至 6.67 升，较 2015 年下降 30% 以上；混合动力车的百公里油耗已降至 4 升。电动汽车技术快速迭代，市场份额、整车产品关键性能及技术指标处于世界先进水平。智能网联汽车整车智能化、网联化水平不断提升，传感器、计算平台、智能座舱等关键软硬件快速更新，高精度地图与定位等基础支撑技术实现了自主突破。车用氢燃料电池技术及相关装备快速发展。质子交换膜制取技术基本实现国产化；双极板技术与产业化能力得到明显提高；金属双极板涂层技术已实现突破，开发了多种具有自主知识产权的石墨基、钛铬基纳米复合涂层，为氢燃料电池汽车的发展奠定了一定基础。

二、数字化低碳化引领能源技术革命新方向

应对气候变化、极端天气、新冠肺炎疫情等非传统安全风险需求的提升，正在成为引导全球科技创新的重要方向。创新突破新能源技术、新材料和新一代信息技术，既是新一轮全球科技革命和产业变革的主战场，也是应对非传统安全风险的必然选择。中国提出到 2035 年跻身创新型国家前列、到 2050 年成为世界科技强国的宏伟目标，需要充分利用自身的科技优势、产业优势、规模优势，把握全球技术革命新机遇，从点突破，连点成线，全面覆盖。聚焦中国能源技术革命，在国家能源安全新战略和"3060"战略目标的指引下，需要坚定不移地贯彻节约资源和保护环境的基本国策，需要坚定不移地构建清洁低碳、安全高效的能源体系，需要坚定不移地建设以新能源为主体的新型电力系统。为此，充分发挥中国数字技术优势和新能源产业优势，加快能源领域低碳化与数字化技术深度融合，持续深度优化能源结构、提升能源综合效率，是未来中国能源技术革命的主要方向。

（一）世界能源技术发展新趋势

1. 全球应对气候变化的绿色低碳技术发展新趋势

随着全球应对气候变化共识不断深化，世界能源将由传统化石能源为主导转向多元化发展的新格局。传统化石能源在一次能源中的占比将不断下降，由 2018 年的 85% 降至 2050 年的 40% 左右①。预测结果显示，

---

① 资料来源：IEA. 世界能源展望 2020. https：//www. bp. com/content/dam/bp/country-sites/zh _ cn/china/home/reports/bp-energy-outlook/2020/energy-outlook-2020-edition-cn. pdf. pdf。

天然气的消费水平与当前相比变化不大，每年约 3 万亿－4 万亿立方米；到 2050 年石油需求量比 2020 年下降约 50%；煤炭消费也将下降 80%以上。相比而言，清洁能源在一次能源消费中的比重将逐步增加。预计到 2050 年，可再生能源（包括风能、太阳能、地热和生物质能）在一次能源结构的比例将由 2018 年的 5%升至 40%以上，其消费量也将增加 10 倍以上。在技术持续进步、成本不断下降及碳价上涨的大趋势下，预计到 2050 年核能需求量将增长 100%左右，氢能（不包括燃料的非燃烧使用）的占比将达到 7%左右。①

　　未来各种能源技术在勘探、开发、储存、运输、加工、消费等环节有望取得长足进步，技术转化应用水平将全面提升。传统能源技术方面，地下原位改质技术、废弃油田再利用技术等可大幅提升传统油气和非常规油气的开采效率；超超临界燃煤发电技术、先进 IGCC 技术的进步与应用可大大降低供电煤耗②。清洁能源技术方面，风能技术创新主要集中于高功率能量转换器、风力涡轮机等；太阳能技术进展主要包括钙钛矿太阳能电池、太阳能光催化制氢等；水电技术将着力攻克深埋特大隧洞岩爆综合防治技术、隧洞工程设计技术；核电技术重点突破核废料处理、核电站安全技术等；光伏制氢、远洋氢气运输及有机化学氢化法氢气储存运输系统（SPERA）等氢能技术获得积极进展；逐步成熟的地热能勘探技术、高温地热能发电技术有望增加地热能的利用程度③。未来数字技术（如超级计算、AI、大数据分析等）可大大提升能源系统效率，尤其是数字化对可再生能源中具有重大产业变革前景技术的迭代加速作用正在不断凸显。具体而言，基于智慧矿山的最优决策模型，数字技术能有效实现对煤矿设计、生产、运营等各个环节的安全、高效、智能化控制；结合现有石油勘探技术，智能机器人的应用可使之前大量无法开采或者高成本开采的油气资源具有技术经济性；风电技术与数字技术的深入融合，将加强风电机组智能控制和发电功率优化；光伏电站的数字化让资

---

① 基于《世界能源展望 2020》中快速转型情景的测算结果。

② 资料来源：孙旭东，张博，彭苏萍，中国洁净煤技术 2035 发展趋势与战略对策研究，中国工程科学，2020，22（3）：132-140。

③ 资料来源：《世界能源技术创新方向及发展趋势》。

产管理、生产管理、后期运维实现提质增效，提高电站预警、抗风险能力，降低人力成本；专业标准化数据模型的应用，将提高地热能、水能的开发效率；数字化也可大大便利运氢方式的选择，有效提高氢能运输场景的匹配度；数字技术有利于反应堆压力容器性能的在线监测和健康管理，延长核电厂寿命。

2. 欧盟《绿政》推动其数字化、绿色化双转型

长期以来，欧盟积极推动自身经济能源绿色化转型及全球气候变化治理，其绿色低碳技术发展处于全球领先水平。2019年上半年，欧盟计划向创新基金的"2020-2030年规划"投入超过100亿欧元，支持低碳技术研发创新，具体包括以下五个方面：一是可再生能源领域，涵盖了浮动式海上风能发电、下一代风力涡轮机等风能技术，太阳能热发电、有机太阳电池、浮动式光伏装置等太阳能技术，增强型地热能技术，先进生物燃料等生物能技术，潮汐能和波浪能技术等海洋能技术。二是储能领域，包括储热、抽热蓄电、液流电池等产品创新，区块链技术和AI等流程创新，港口能量管理系统和充电站等系统创新，以及电解水耦合储氢系统等大规模示范项目。三是碳捕集、利用与封存（CCUS）领域，包含全周期碳捕集与封存（CCS）项目、部分环节CCS项目、捕集二氧化碳和其他含碳排放气体并转化为可用的燃料或产品等低碳技术创新。四是能源密集型工业领域，涵盖焦炭、炼油、金属、玻璃、水泥、化学制品及其他行业各生产环节的低碳技术创新。五是交叉领域，包括多工厂CCUS、低碳氢的利用、混合可再生能源系统，以及热泵工业加热系统等低碳技术创新。

在此基础上，2019年12月，欧盟发布了《欧洲绿色政纲》（简称《绿政》），确立了2030年温室气体排放量在1990年基础上减少50%-55%的阶段性目标，以及实现2050年气候中性的长期目标。《绿政》是欧盟中长期可持续增长的综合性经济战略，进一步明确了欧盟未来发展能源、工业、交通、建筑、生物多样性等七大发展领域及重点任务。能源领域包括发展可再生能源、淘汰煤电、建设智慧能源设施等；工业领域包括加快能源密集型行业脱碳、大力支持氢能等突破性技术研发商用、

推动电池行业战略价值链投资和发展可持续数字产业等；建筑领域包括提高建筑改造率、探索建筑碳排放交易体系和开展建筑能源绩效合同管理等；交通领域包括发展多式联运、建设智能交通系统、提高船舶和飞机等的空气污染物排放和二氧化碳排放标准等；食品领域包括进行农业生态绩效考核、减少农药化肥使用和加强食品全供应链管控等；生态领域包括出台加强生物多样性立法、欧盟森林战略和发展可持续"蓝色经济"，实施空气、水和土壤零污染行动，开展可持续化学品管理等。其中，欧盟《绿政》更注重各领域绿色低碳技术与数字技术的智能融合，充分挖掘数字转型的潜力，加快 AI、5G、云计算和边缘计算及物联网等数字技术在能源技术领域应用。尽管因新冠肺炎疫情影响，《绿政》相关的工作安排受到干扰，但欧盟始终将《绿政》中数字基础设施、清洁能源、循环经济、智能交通系统等战略性投资作为疫情后恢复经济的"马歇尔欧洲计划"的重要内容。欧盟也将出台投融资、财政等系列绿色政策加以配合，如加大绿色投资、扩大绿色融资及推行绿色财政，以确保《绿政》的推行与实施。

　　未来欧盟将从数字化与绿色化两个方向共同发力，进一步推动欧洲乃至全球低碳技术研发创新与应用，实现其气候目标任务。

3. 美国碳中和战略推动电动汽车等新能源技术加快发展

　　作为世界最大经济体，早在 2007 年美国二氧化碳排放便已达峰（60.03 亿吨），2019 年美国能源消耗产生的二氧化碳排放量已降至 51.46 亿吨，2020 年进一步减少至 45.74 亿吨。美国总统拜登上台后积极寻求美在全球气候谈判中的领导作用，就职后即签署行政令重返《巴黎协定》，并于 2021 年 4 月 22 日的领导人气候峰会上宣布了美方新的气候承诺：2030 年温室气体排放比 2005 年水平减少 50%-52%。与此同时，美国政府提出"到 2035 年，通过向可再生能源过渡实现无碳发电；到 2050 年，让美国实现碳中和"。

　　多年来，美国政府重视电动汽车等新能源技术的研发投资，美能源部曾先后多次、大量投资电动汽车研发项目，包括自由合作汽车研究计划、新一代汽车伙伴计划、先进能源计划、先进技术汽车制造贷款计划等，支持研发动力电池、燃料电池、轻量化等技术。同时，为最大限度地减少电动汽车行业中的能源消耗和浪费，美国还推动建立了动力电池回收利用网络。2019年，美国能源部设立了第一个锂离子电池回收中心，橡树岭国家实验室、阿贡实验室等科研机构和企业参与其中，共同推动了废旧动力电池的闭环回收与利用。

未来美国将继续大力发展低碳技术，推动电动汽车等新能源技术发展。一方面，美国政府计划对清洁能源与可持续基础设施领域投资2万亿美元；投入1.28亿美元以降低太阳能发电成本、发展太阳能发电技术；投资4000亿美元支持清洁能源研发和创新，并计划设立专注于气候变化的跨机构高级研究机构ARPA-C（ARPA-Climate），加大对清洁能源研究与创新资金支持力度，加倍对CCUS技术的联邦投资，加快CCUS等技术开发和应用。而且美国政府还设立了"清洁能源和可持续加速器"项目，动员私人部门资金参与可再生能源发电等领域投资。另一方面，美国主要聚焦于电动汽车、电网建设和可再生能源等领域。首先，美国政府计划重组工厂并增加国内材料供应、对电动汽车购买者实施税收优惠、改造电动校车并在全国范围内建设50万座电动车充电站。其次，美国政府将建设一个更有弹性的电网，加大对风能、太阳能和其他可再生能源项目的税收优惠，积极推进公共土地和近海水域的可再生能源生产，计划至2030年将海上风电装机翻一番；再次，为提高能效、降低碳排放，美国政府将着力改造并升级学校、办公楼、住宅等建筑，推动绿色建筑发展，助力减污降碳。

（二）中国能源技术发展愿景

1. 能源低碳转型发展

中国与发达国家的经济社会发展阶段不同，能源资源禀赋不同，存在资源时空分布与用能需求发展不均衡等现实问题，未来中国能源革命不会也不能重复发达国家的能源发展路线，必将以多元能源发展为方向，完成从以煤炭为主向以非化石能源为主的绿色、低碳、安全、高效能源体系转型发展。这是中国能源革命的必然选择，也给能源技术革命带来巨大挑战。为此，需要能源技术革命推动能源新技术、新能源技术加快突破，充分发挥数字技术优势，实现数字化与低碳化深度融合。

未来在"3060"战略目标指引下，中国能源技术革命向绿色低碳发展的方向更加清晰、步伐更加稳健，推动能源基础理论、技术链条和产业形态等加速突破。在2030年前实现二氧化碳达峰阶段，传统能源领域将继续推动新的技术攻关，如超高水头超低水头水轮机设计，燃气轮机高温先进材料、重型燃气轮机和单循环小型燃气轮机研发，煤电高效低成本CCUS技术，小型模块化反应堆、快堆、熔盐堆等新一代先进核电技术。新能源领域技术将大力发展，如高效低成本晶体硅电池产业化技术，高参数太阳能热发电技术，大型风电关键技术设备，远海大型风电系统设计与建设技术，低成本中低风速风力发电技术，燃料电池分布式发电技术，潮汐能发电技术，干热岩发电技术等，以及高精度、长尺度新能源功率预测技术，高比例分布式新能源状态感知与调控技术等，将推动新能源从补充角色迅速成长为主体能源之一，满足绝大部分新增能源需求。

在2060年前实现碳中和阶段，中国能源技术革命向纵深迈进，将引导创立新的绿色能源知识和技术体系。以"互联网+"智慧能源为基本架构的能源技术体系将基本建成，形成以"可再生能源+灵活性资源"为主的电能供应技术体系，和以化石能源清洁高效利用、CCUS和氢能为主的非电供应技术体系。为此，需要继续推动储能技术快速迭代，为可再生能源和电动汽车快速发展提供有力支撑；加快突破氢能产业链的核心关键技术和装备；发挥举国体制机制优势，实现CCUS技术的国产化和产业化，高效回收利用工业领域、建筑领域、交通领域的碳排放，结合碳汇实现碳中和目标。

2. 关键技术发展

（1）可再生与新能源领域技术

预计到2030年，中国一次能源需求将进入峰值平台期，能源结构加速优化，非化石能源将在 2035 年后超过煤炭成为利用规模最大的一次能源，到 2050 年占一次能源需求总量的 2/3 以上。太阳能、风能、生物质能、地热能、潮汐能、第三代和第四代核能等新能源产业规模的不断扩张，将持续推进新能源技术及装备的创新发展。

具体而言，太阳能技术研究重点关注钙钛矿太阳能电池、叠层太阳能电池、太阳能光催化制氢、催化剂、半导体电极等。风能技术研究的主要热点包括高功率能量转换器、风力涡轮机、风电数值模拟、风电高比例稳定并网等。生物质能技术研究主要关注木质素热解、催化剂、预处理、微藻生物燃料、生物精炼、纤维素生物燃料等方向。储能技术研究主要聚焦锂离子电池、钠离子电池、锂硫电池、正负极材料、快充技术等方向。地热能技术研究热点方向包括增强型地热系统、地热系统数值模拟、地热钻井技术等。核能技术研究主要关注核废料处理技术、核电站安全技术、耐辐照材料、小型核反应堆技术等。

（2）新型电力系统

新型电力系统是以新能源为生产、消费主体，多种电网形态协同发展，具有绿色低碳、多元互动、柔性灵活、协同高效、数字智能、安全可控等特征的电力系统。在中国能源革命的推动下，分布式新能源和电动汽车快速发展，加速配电、用电形态变化进程，大量电力电子设备入网，系统惯量大幅降低，安全稳定运行面临巨大挑战。为此，新型电力系统在技术上将重点围绕两个方面开展研究突破。

一是走多能融合、多网融合的发展路径。新型电力系统将以因地制宜的多元能源结构为基础，氢能、储能等新技术规模化应用，电能、热能、冷能协同互补、相互支撑，做到"大基地+大电网"与"分布式+微电网"并举，实现多种能源基础设施网络高度融合。在供给侧，高比例新能源广泛接入，跨域资源需要实现灵活可靠配置，以满足各类分布式能源设施平稳接入；在需求侧，峰谷差和波动性加大，同时用户既是能源的产消者，也是电力平衡的参与者。这要求系统内的源网荷储深度协同互动，从"源随荷动"向"荷随源动"与"源荷互动"转变，实现"横向多能互融，纵向协同发力"。

二是推动先进数字技术与能源技术高度融合。突破高比例新能源和高比例电力电子设备的电力系统稳定控制、风险决策基础理论，全面建成新能源功率预测水平大幅提升、适应新能源特点的智能化调度体系。通过系统数字化、网络化和智能化，推动多种能源高度融合，大幅提升电力电子设备的灵活可控性，有效应对电力系统不确定性，提高电力系统安全防御能力。深度挖掘需求侧响应潜力，源网荷储系统整体优化，做到电力系统的广泛互联和智能互动。通过构建开放共享、协同高效的现代能源服务数字化平台，实现"能源结构生态化、产能用能一体化、资源配置高效化"。

（3）氢能领域技术

氢能是一种来源广泛、清洁灵活、应用场景丰富的二次能源。氢能技术包括基础材料科学、设备制造、基础设施建设等一系列综合性技术。目前氢能产业发展仍处于早期阶段，需重点关注三个领域。

氢能制取存在三条技术路线：传统化石能源制氢的"灰氢"路线将受到限制，利用湿法炼焦、氯碱和丙烷脱氢等技术生产工业副产氢或将得到重视；化石能源制氢与 CCUS 技术结合的"蓝氢"路线有望成为制氢的重要方式；利用可再生能源制备氢气的"绿氢"路线是未来氢能发展的主要方向，包括碱性水电解技术、质子交换膜水电解技术、固体氧化物水电解技术，并正在探索太阳能光热制氢、核能制氢等非电解制氢路线。

储氢和运氢环节仍需要攻克诸多难题，高效低耗的氢气储运技术是未来科研攻关的重点方向。一方面，目前高压气态储氢技术基本成熟，正在研发更优性能的高压容器材料，提高压力等级，减轻罐体重量；低温液态储氢将重点研发高效保温容器和液化低能耗技术和装备；有机液态储氢需攻克低成本、低功耗脱氢催化剂；固体材料储氢要突破低熔点储氢介质，大幅提高储氢质量、效率指标。另一方面，管道输氢仍面临材料氢脆等难题，正在开展天然气掺氢的管输实验，未来或将以此方式实现大规模间接输氢。

氢能在终端利用领域的技术仍需突破。一方面，氢燃料电池有望成为未来交通、建筑用能的重要方式，燃料电池可为大功率交通设备提供清洁动力，利用燃料电池也可参与热电联供与电力调峰，有助于实现多能源系统的协调优化运行。而且，氢能作为燃料的内燃机技术，特别是航空燃料技术，也将展开相关研发和应用。另一方面，氢在冶金、化工领域的需求空间可望大幅增长，氢作为还原剂替代焦炭炼铁的相关技术，以及作为化工原料消纳二氧化碳等技术，正在试验和推广应用。

（4）CCUS 领域技术

CCUS 技术是指将人为产生的二氧化碳，使用一定的方式捕集并运输到特定地点，加以利用或封存的技术。预计到 2060 年，中国仍将排放 15 亿吨左右二氧化碳，需要通过 CCUS 技术在 2060 年实现碳中和。

CCUS 技术目前最先进和被最广泛采用的是化学吸收（如乙醇胺化合物）和物理分离（吸附剂通过温度或压力变化释放）。其中，从烟气流中分离或捕集二氧化碳的技术已商业化，水泥、煤化工、石油化工、炼焦、整体煤气化联合循环发电系统等工业尾气二氧化碳捕集效果较好。随着高二氧化碳选择性的聚合物或无机装置（膜）技术被逐步攻克，低浓度电厂烟道气二氧化碳捕集技术有望大规模应用。

二氧化碳地质封存技术包括咸水层封存、煤层封存、海洋封存等技术。从钻井到注入、从静态评价到动态模拟，通过智能选区选址、智能注采、实时监测等智能化技术，实现安全、环保的智能封存。具体而言，在将二氧化碳压缩注入特定地质条件的岩石构造（废弃油气田、深部难开采煤层、深层地下水层等地质环境）前，要经过静态建模、地质力学建模，以及动态数模技术进行精细模拟与评价；针对二氧化碳埋存特性，进行选区选址、注采运行模拟；分析盖层完整性与断层激活风险评估、井筒完整性评价等工作。

二氧化碳利用技术主要包括油气增产技术和化工领域技术。一方面，油气增产技术通过智能化注气设备、油气压裂装备，提高油藏压力和原油流动性，实现二氧化碳压裂、二氧化碳驱油气，同时实现二氧化碳部分封存。另一方面，二氧化碳生产可降解塑料、二氧化碳结合绿氢生产化肥和其他石化产品等相关技术有望得到广泛应用，生产生物油品与饲料研发等微藻固碳技术具有较好的应用前景。

（三）数字化低碳化融合的重点技术方向

以建设清洁低碳、智慧高效、经济安全的能源体系为目标，通过传统能源新技术与数字技术的逐步融合，在智慧无人矿山、智慧油田、智慧工厂、智慧储运等技术领域加快突破，促进传统化石能源向绿色低碳方向转型；通过将新能源技术与数字化、智能化技术深度融合，在智慧发电、智慧电网、智慧储电、智慧用电等技术领域持续发力，构建以新能源为主体的新型电力系统，促使可再生能源占比增加，逐步提高能源综合效率，进一步提升能源系统运行安全水平，形成多能融合、产供储销协同的智慧能源系统。

1. 数字技术

在新发展阶段，数据作为新生产要素，与资本、人力、能源资源等要素相结合，推动能源产业数字化发展。利用数字技术、通信技术、AI技术等新一代信息技术与能源技术融合创新，着力解决能源领域的粗放式、低效率、高污染、高碳排问题。该领域以研究咨询、架构设计、数据治理和技术方案着手，通过智能感知、边缘计算、智能联接、智慧平台和智慧应用等先进技术应用，使能源领域形成多种能源耦合和多种能源数据融合的新业态，适用于各类能源生产、加工、输送、存储和消费，以及碳管理与交易等全业务场景。

（1）智能感知与云边协同

智能感知技术利用先进传感技术将能源现场环境信息转换成数字量，智能终端对数字量进行处理计算后通过网络传输给平台。智能感知与云边协同解决各种能源环境下信息的采集、传输和处理等关键问题。

传感器技术。能源传感器将生产、传输、存储和消费环节的特征参数、环境和人为特征等转换成电信号和数字量，具有感知机理复杂多样的特点。能源传感器在复杂的环境中运行，有各种强干扰信号，对低功耗、运行寿命提出较高的要求。需要解决不同传感器的材料、微观结构、制作工艺性能、数字化处理、表面修饰，以及可靠性、耐候性和低功耗等技术问题，研究各种新型传感材料、感知机理和高精度传感元器件及其组成的器件。能源传感器应用于化石能源的勘查、开采、输送和消费，以及发电、输电、变电、配电、用电等场景。对无法安装传感器的场景，可采取视频图像分析等手段获取感知信息。

微源取能。将太阳能、风能、热能、机械振动、电能等微能量进行转换，因地制宜为传感器和传感网络供电。具有集成度高，多种技术融合的特点。需要解决自供能传感器电源性能、电池性能及安全性技术问题，对电磁兼容设计、封装集成、结构设计及延寿措施等一系列技术开展研究。微源取能与传感器和传感网络集成一起安装于有光照、风力、振动、热能、电能等场所。

低功耗无线传感网络。无线传感网络具有长距离广域覆盖、星型组网和中短距离局域覆盖、自组多跳网络转发两种典型通信方式，前者传输速率低、部署成本低、终端接入量高，长距离覆盖和低工作功率兼顾；后者传输速率高、传输距离短、接入量低、功率低、抗干扰性能强，需配置轻量级的网关和协议。需要解决传感器网络的低（超低）功耗、传感器在线率，以及传感器网络免维护和少维护等问题，研究传感器及传感网的硬件节能设计和软件设计方法、超低能耗的节点节能运行策略和网络传输的节能策略，以及无线通讯发射功率的控制技术。低功耗广域网络适用于各类能源现场数据传输场景，广泛应用于矿山、油气田、电厂电网等领域，尤其是环境恶劣、人工成本高的场景。

边缘智能终端。在有些场景，通信技术在时延、带宽方面存在不足，使得云平台侧计算能力与终端侧计算需求不能匹配，要通过边缘计算将云计算的能力下沉到终端节点，实现终端侧的智能化。需要进一步解决边缘计算、存储、安全和云边协同等问题，研究能源传感器网络的状态表征、信息模型、标识定位、多维感知数据融合分析等技术，适用于时延和带宽敏感的复杂计算场景。

（2）智能联接

智慧终端和智慧平台之间的数据传输网络将以更高速率和更高服务

等级协议（SLA）服务水平传输业务数据，5G、F5G、IPv6+智慧网络管理及其他通信技术组合可满足全场景的能源数据传输需求，在低时延、可靠性和安全性等方面做到无缝覆盖。未来需要解决各种网络接入和网络智慧管理，以及能源海量数据的传输、安全、时效问题。

智能通信网络管理。通过融合通信网络管理控制技术、平台技术、终端技术和 AI 等技术，对通信网络进行监控，自动配置网络资源、调整数据路径，快速预测、分析和排除网络故障，评估网络安全和性能，实现通信网络规划、建设、运行、维护的智能化，跨地域、跨网络的分级通信网络管理，以及海量终端广泛接入和 SLA 保障。需要解决能源海量网元和终端的接入、管理、安全、运维等问题，适用于对 SLA 保障和可靠性要求高的数据传输通信网络运行场景。

5G 通信技术。具有高指向性传输、高增益、强抗干扰等性能，可消除多重干扰，实现载波间隔等参数的灵活配置，提升系统容量，提供端到端的业务安全隔离，以及面向用户和业务的差异化端到端服务体验。峰值速率超过每秒 20 千兆比特、通信时延小于 1 毫秒、每平方千米支持 100 万个设备接入，具有高速率、大带宽、低时延、大容量、高移动性、广域覆盖、高密度等技术特点，在频谱、技术性能指标等方面能够满足各种行业应用需求。需要解决能源海量数据的无线传输、安全、时效等问题，可广泛应用于智慧矿山、智慧油田、智能电网、智能工厂、零碳园区等场景。

F5G 技术。基于光传送网（OTN）、千兆比无源光网络（GPON）/十千兆比无源光网络（XGPON）等光传送技术，光时域反射仪（OTDR）、光纤质量监控/光性能监控（FD/OD）等光纤维护技术，和光纤传感（震动、温度，偏移）技术/光纤监测技术等组成的技术体系，是新一代全光固定网络通信技术的总称，具有更强的多业务承载能力、更高的稳定性、安全性和可靠性。需要进一步解决工业互联网的大带宽（每秒 2 兆-100 千兆比特）、低时延（50 毫秒）、高可靠（环网保护）、无源远距离接入、防爆等应用问题，将应用于未来光通信基础承载网络中，可适用于煤矿井下长距离无源工业光环网通信、油气管道光纤安全预警、电网信息通信主干网络等场景。

"IPv6+"通信技术。"IPv6+"是网际互连协议（IP）数据承载网在面向 5G/物联网时代的一系列创新协议的集合，包括基于 IPv6 转发平面的分段路由（SRv6）、网络分片、端到端传输质量检测、智能流量调优等典型技术，是智能化、简单化、自动化、SLA 可承诺的下一代承载网。补充了 IP 协议的短板，需要解决场景实际应用中的网络传输时延、抖动、丢包等问题，实现传输过程中的可靠性承诺，在各能源企业生产网、办公网中将得到广泛应用。

（3）智慧平台

智慧平台依托于能源数据和智慧应用，提供计算与存储、云平台和能源公共云服务等信息技术（IT）基础设施和组件，为生产运行提供必要的手段，助力能源行业的提质增效和价值创造，支持产业链和生态圈的创新发展。需要解决平台架构、IT 公共服务、能源公共云服务等问题。

计算技术。计算技术的发展将不断提升中央处理器（CPU）处理速度、数值计算能力和集成度，并通过对服务器本身的智能化，突破 CPU 对服务器算力带来的瓶颈，实现对不同负载（Workload）提供高效的算力。经典计算技术将以现有的速度和规模不断发展，并将遇到瓶颈，需要探索和研究突破性计算技术，如量子计算等技术。

数据存储技术。作为智慧能源基础设施中的重要组成，通过提升单位空间和能耗下的存储密度，提升数据读写性能和处理效率，提供更安全的数据存储方案，让数据存得下、用得好、安全可信。具备大带宽、低时延、高存储密度、高可靠性、大容量等技术特点，数据访问带宽达到 PB 级，访问时延达到 μs 级，数据存储量达到 ZB 级，数据可靠性达到 99.9999%，故障场景下业务不中断、数据不丢失，能够满足各种行业应用的存储需求。需要进一步解决海量数据的存放成本、读取效率、数据可靠性、数据安全性问题。

云平台。基于 IT 硬件资源和软件资源的服务，提供计算、网络和存储能力，具有低成本、规模化、弹性扩容、高可靠等特点，是能源行业的数字基础设施底座。平台的响应速度加快，平台数据算力、算法和应用等基础支撑能力更加共享化和服务化，并兼顾安全性和抗冲击能力；

平台的架构多样，可提供模型工具、数据质量管理工具和故障分析工具，能够将应用快速转变为服务。需要解决公有云和私有云等多种云的无缝同步、数据全域互通、面向开放共享的数据安全与隐私保护、安全监测与攻防对抗等技术问题，开发数据模型、数据治理和数据质量管理等工具，进一步提升系统资源的协同调度、公共服务和开发模式等。

能源公共云服务。平台即服务（PaaS）、软件即服务（SaaS）、数据处理、行业模型等是能源公共云服务的关键要素，可支撑快速接入大数据、AI、区块链等智慧应用。能源数据的大规模接入和业务数据及应用的全域共享是公共云服务的基本要素，要求能源数据在建设、管理、运行、维护等环节打通，消除数据孤岛、划清数据安全边界、统一数据模型。需要解决公共云服务快速建设和响应、能源数据大规模接入和数据与应用共享、数据集成与应用的快速交付以及支撑工具等问题，并研究能源数据模型、数字孪生信息模型、实景与实体建模与重构等数据模型。

（4）智慧应用

智慧应用依托于平台与数据，利用 AI、大数据、区块链等技术，通过机器人、无人机和智能分析等，进行运行控制与管理，实现价值创造。需要解决机器认知学习、逻辑推理和智能决策等问题。

大数据应用。基于先进信息技术，对多维度、海量数据进行提取、处理、加工和关联关系等分析，揭示能源与经济、环境、民生等内在规律，及时快速反馈分析结果，协助处理能源生产运维、市场交易所需要的信息，助力政府监管和企业管理决策。需要解决数据孤岛多、标准不统一、海量级大数据处理难、模型适用性差等问题，适用于行业景气指数、城市负荷热点、用户信用与价值分析、行业发展趋势等一系列跨行业跨领域数据分析场景。

人工智能应用。结合机器人、无人机、影像智能识别、辅助决策支持等技术，改变传统能源生产运行模式，使部分能源生产控制运行系统具有自主分析、自主控制、自主决策等自主作业的智能行为方式。需要解决机器代替人工进行作业、分析、控制和决策等问题，研究能源领域知识图谱及认知推理，以及智能认知、智能控制决策和融合群体智能与人机优化决策等，可用于输电网、长输管网无人机巡检和矿山井下机器人作业、电网高空作业、水下钻井机器人、救援机器人等高危人工作业场景。

区块链应用。能源区块链是应用于能源行业的一种分布式记账方式，以安全透明的方式进行交易和记录，任意节点的活动受其他节点的监督，无法伪装欺诈，可匿名交换数据而无需彼此的身份和个人信息。需要解决能源数据真实性和安全性以及能源交易中的不可篡改等问题，适用于分布式能源交易、能源资产交易、碳管理与交易等场景。

2. 智慧能源技术

未来能源绿色低碳转型发展要求加快能源技术变革，推动能源新技术、新能源技术与先进信息通信技术等深度融合，逐步形成智能化的能源生产、加工、输送、存储和利用技术体系，促使化石能源产供储销体系更为智能和完善，非化石能源"源网荷储"更加智慧和协同，新能源在能源系统中的占比逐步提升到50%以上，能源综合利用效率不断提升，节能减排效果继续提高，为能源生产和消费变革提供有力的技术支撑。

（1）智慧发电

智慧发电技术系统通过发电技术与新一代数字技术深度融合，具有高水平自动控制出力、远程监控、维护便捷等特征，可在一定范围内提高匹配电力需求的灵活性，更适合未来构建以新能源为主体的新型电力系统。但新能源发电存在波动性强、受天气影响大、低惯性等特点，容易引发出力随机、与需求负荷峰值难以匹配等问题，需要研究进一步提升可再生能源效率、平抑新能源出力波动性、提高电源侧出力可靠性和稳定性等技术。

智慧光伏电站技术。智慧光伏电站由智能光伏组件、智能组串式逆变器、智慧光伏控制器、智慧运维云中心等组成，具有新能源发电功率预测、智能监控系统、智能电流电压（IV）诊断、AI机器学习、机器人智能清洗、无人机智能巡检等特点。需要解决光伏电站在多应用场景、复杂地形环境下，进一步提升转化效率、无人化水平、与气象大数据深度融合，以及光伏电站出力和弃光消纳问题。适用于山地、水上漂浮电站及水面等人工检测组件难度大、成本高的场景，可降低光伏电站的选址要求。

智慧风电场技术。具有智能设计、场群集中监控、智能故障诊断、大数据预测预警、预防性维护、增强现实（AR）巡检、端对端的场群绩效管理等功能，有抗扰性、自适应性、经济性的特点。需要解决复杂地形、低速、高空及海上风电的远程运维问题，以识别风电损失电量因素，进一步提升发电量可利用率、提高风场运营效率、降低发电成本。可应用于丘陵和山顶等复杂地形，低风速、高海拔、低温等特殊环境，陆上及海上风电场的选址、装配、安装、维修和运行等环节。

智慧核电技术。使用智能诊断分析算法，对关键设备开展智能诊断分析、提出运维策略，具有一体化、智能化、少人化、安全化等特点。需要解决复杂工况下不能及时对核电站故障做出正确判断、采取正确措施导致严重安全事故等问题，可在复杂环境下自动预报、发现、诊断、预测和提出建议，显著提高核电站的安全性和可用度，应用于抵御海啸、外部洪水、大型飞机撞击等极端场景。

（2）智慧电网

智慧电网技术通过深度融合物理电网和数字电网，具有电力和信息的双向流动性、高度自动化、高灵活性、信息实时交换等特征。可有效解决高度电力电子化带来的稳定机理变化，以及高比例新能源接入、终端高度电气化和分散化的负荷带来的系统稳定运行难题，以及电力市场价格波动等问题，进一步提升供电的安全性、可靠性、灵活性，提高电能质量及能源效率。

智慧输电技术。通过小微智能传感器、物联感知终端、AI 平台等技术与电力电子技术相互融合与应用，使位于偏远地区的关键输电设施处于数字化实时感知和调控状态下，实现数字化动态本体孪生，可改变输电网络的信息形态，具有智能化、数据驱动、抗干扰、全景看、全息判、全程控等特征。需要解决数字形态下故障快速定位、诊断、恢复，全天候的无人化巡检、少人化抢修，以及 AI 智能巡检存在识别率不高、供电难、抗干扰能力弱、受环境影响大等问题，适用于跨域度广、地形气候条件复杂、传输能力强的输电网络。

智慧变电技术。成为多种能源交互的枢纽，对交互关联的能源与电网实现多维度感知、分析和决策，执行无人化智能操作，具有数字化平台与多系统多终端融合统一、一二次设备融合、软件定义终端、远程在线升级、设备状态实时感知等特征。通过数字化技术与柔性直流技术的融合，可处理大规模新能源接入出现的电压不稳、宽频震荡、惯量减小、频率不稳等状况。需要解决全息实时信息便捷获得、海量数据快速有效分析和运维检修智能决策等问题，适用于新能源大规模接入和大型城市综合能源柔性互联、海洋孤岛和平台供电等场景。

智慧配电技术。通过边缘计算终端、本地数据存储、计算与分析等技术手段，实现低功耗、广覆盖、低成本、生命周期免维护等目标，具有电力电子化比例大、网络结构复杂多元、多源供电网络、能源双向流动和馈线组能源互济等特征。需要进一步解决分布式能源调控、设备全生命周期监控、故障自诊断自修复、孤岛效应、电能质量治理、需求响应等问题，提升配电网设备在线状态检测、配网运维巡检智能化水平，打造安全可靠、绿色高效的智慧配电网络，构建面向未来源网荷储四维融合互动的新型配网系统。

智慧调度运行技术。针对大规模可再生能源出力不可控、波动性强等特性，智慧调度管理对象从电力系统的电源、输电侧转向配电负荷侧，挖掘并利用大量分布式灵活性资源，通过态势感知、数字孪生实现源网荷协同，具有合规性、精细化、信息透明等特点。需要解决实时统筹调度、源网荷储协同互动、功率平衡、平滑波动、减少故障等问题。

虚拟电厂技术。通过量测技术、调控技术、通信技术实现地理位置分散的各种分布式资源的聚合和协调优化，可参与电力市场和辅助服务市场运行，为配电网和输电网提供管理和辅助服务。需要解决分布式资源调度难等问题，可有效缓解局部地区装机容量不足的矛盾。虚拟电厂按功能不同，可划分为商业型虚拟电厂和技术型虚拟电厂。商业型虚拟电厂不考虑虚拟电厂对配电网的影响，并以与传统发电厂类似的方式加入电力市场。技术型虚拟电厂是从系统管理角度出发，考虑聚合资源对本地网络的实时影响。

（3）智慧储电

智慧储电技术通过存储虚拟化、精细控制等一系列技术，可与新能源场站、变电站、新型负荷等联合运行，具有快速充放电、灵活智能、标准化、模块化、软件可定义等特征。需要解决新能源随机性、间歇性和不稳定性对电力系统的影响及储能系统安全性、兼容性等问题，以提高发电设备利用率、协助电网调峰、增强配电网的可控性、提高电网稳定性，支撑新能源并网消纳。

智慧光储技术。AI、云计算技术与光伏及智能组串式储能深度融合，智能组串式储能技术基于分布式储能系统架构，采用电池模组级能量优化、电池单簇能量控制、数字智能化管理、全模块化设计等技术，实现电池模组一包一优化、一簇一管理的精细化管控，在更多放电的同时降低储能平准化成本。具有组串化、智能化、模块化等技术特征，有经济高效、安全可靠、智能运维、寿命较长的特点，需要进一步解决大规模可再生能源接入电网、提升供电质量、电网调峰及安全运行等问题，适用于地面电站、家庭绿电、行业绿电、海岛离网等多种场景。

智慧抽水蓄能电站。采集抽水蓄能电站勘测设计、土建施工、机电安装和运行维护环节全生命周期的数据进行智能化管理，实现信息数字化、通信网络化、集成标准化、运管一体化、业务互动化、运行最优化、决策智能化，提升机组的智能化建设和运维水平，支撑电站从计划检修模式向柔性状态检修模式转变，具有响应速度快、功率调节快、运行方式灵活、安全等级高的特点。需要进一步解决电站建设运维缺陷隐患、运行安全风险等问题，促进清洁能源消纳。

云储能技术。应用数据分析、优化、预测等多种技术，将分散在用户侧的储能装置集中到云端，统一调度、统一维护，用云端的虚拟储能容量来代替电网调度或用户侧的实体储能。云储能基于电网，将共享经济与电力系统深入融合，具有虚拟化、共享化、一致性和可传输性特点。需要解决最大限度共享储能资源、电网或用户不必再专门购买储能装置等问题，以提高现有的闲置储能的利用率，聚拢大量的具有互补性的用户并实现规模效益。

（4）智慧用电

智慧用电技术通过准确及时采集相关信息、分析用电数据、了解用户用电行为和用电状态、提高电能数据信息的统计效率和质量，提升用电效率、节能减排，具有智能计量、智能采集、高速通信、终端交互等特征。需要进一步解决电气安全隐患、削峰填谷、系统效率低等问题，实现负荷多元互动、高度电气化、需求快速响应等目标。需求侧响应是改变用户用能方式的一种机制，通过市场价格信号或者激励机制调整用户用能行为，以有效抑制电网波动。

光储充直柔建筑一体化技术。推动电力负载由刚性转为柔性、驱动方式由交流转为直流、建筑从电能消费者转为产消者，具有综合性、高效性、灵活性等特征。需要进一步解决光伏发电和建筑用电系统不断进行交流和直流转换、重复接入转换装置造成的能量损失等问题。其中"光伏+直流+智能充电桩"技术可降低中低压电网输配电的容量，带储能的直流用电建筑可提升能源利用效率。

电动汽车车辆到电网（V2G）技术。V2G是电动汽车与电网双向互动技术，包括电动汽车充电技术、电池向电网放电技术、智能电网与电动汽车互联互通协同技术等。电动汽车作为临时移动式、分布式的储能设施，通过有序充放电实现削峰填谷，在用电高峰时给电网供电、在低谷时从电网充电，可有效提高电网运行效率和资源配置能力。

绿色智慧数据中心用电技术。基于直流配电、不间断电源（UPS）按需配置、电池智能管理等技术，可降低数据中心能耗、简化管理、降低成本，与可再生能源供电方案、需求侧管理等技术结合，增加可再生能源用电量，平抑电网的波动。借助模块化数据中心方案和资源融合特性，可大大降低物理空间占用率，有效降低综合能耗和电能利用效率（PUE）；智能运维平台可实现从全景监测到自动化监控，从基于规则的故障发现到基于AI机器学习的故障预知。

（5）智慧油气勘探开发

油气勘探开发应用智能传感、智能类比、知识图谱、机器学习等技术，构建油藏地质、工程、生产一体化作业模型，通过海量的样本数据进行深度学习训练，实现储层物性信息的快速智能识别和评价、钻完井工程设计与施工的实时跟踪和智能监测、井筒工程事故智能诊断与预警等。需要解决油气勘探开发各专业领域数据条块分割、软件碎片化、AI算法适配等问题，满足上游业务全链条智能化的发展需求。

智慧油气勘探技术。利用盆地模拟、智能地球物理勘探及智能钻、测、录井技术，结合智能勘探评价与决策系统，实时精确识别及精细描述前景油气储层，准确预测油气资源空间分布，精细评价盆地资源、科学定量评估潜在油气藏及预期储量规模。需要解决海量数据的样本不准确、不全等机器学习难以有效应用等问题，满足智慧油气田勘探的需求，全面实现一体化地质精细评价及资源预测。

智慧油气开发技术。利用蚁群算法、粒子群算法等智能算法技术，运用数字孪生、远传控制、千万级网格的超高精度数模技术等，通过多专业系统设计，实时抓取生产动态数据，综合考虑储量动用率、油气藏采收率、开发效益等核心指标，实现对井筒和地面工艺在线模拟、直观展示与动态调参、开发方案实时调整与智能优化。预计到2030年形成智慧油气开发技术系列。

智慧成井技术。利用遗传算法、随机森林、人工神经网络等AI智慧成井技术，满足数据全方位采集与深度挖掘、地面和井下装备实时闭环控制、钻完井智能决策等技术要求。以解决传统钻完井工程理论与AI技术的跨界融合问题，实现钻井导向、轨迹控制、参数优化的全面智能化。

（6）智慧油气储运

智慧油气储运利用工业大数据技术、数字孪生等智能技术，深度挖掘线路和站场设备的检测、监测、失效等大量数据，构建储运系统数字化孪生体，形成可智能监测、预测的智能化技术体系。需要解决储运系统点多、线长、面广、设备多元特征带来的管道运行状况、外部环境约束、资源和市场等难以准确研判问题，满足油气储运系统智能管理、设备监测、事故预测和诊断等方面的需求，实现储运系统高效安全运行。

智慧油气管网技术。通过构建不同层级油气管网系统的数字孪生体，形成智能优化、运行的管网管理技术体系，做到多层级油气管网统一智能化建设，具备全方位感知、综合性预判、自适应优化、一体化管控的油气管网系统数字化和智能化能力，并可动态适应外部环境、资源市场的变化。需要解决智能油气管网数字孪生体构建、知识模型的结构及内容确定等问题。2030年，实现油气管网全面智能化管理、运行、监测、预测及诊断。

智慧油气储存技术。通过制修订各类油气储存系统的数字化、智能化相关标准，形成地下储库及罐体的智能化管理及技术体系，结合虚拟生产环境对真实生产环境的映射，建立具有优化、预测及决策的智能化油气储存技术体系。需要解决数据获取困难、机理模型复杂等机器学习融入知识模型困难等问题，满足智能优化库存、智能维护、智能调峰等需要。

智慧液化天然气储运技术。通过液化天然气接收、储存、气化、外输及与天然气管网互联互通数字化的基础上，利用多种AI技术，建立智慧远程决策支持中心，使得生产实时响应资源和市场变化，实现从液化天然气（LNG）接收、储存到气化、外输LNG整个储运系统的协同优化。需要解决LNG系统全过程智能控制技术和LNG储运理论与AI技术交叉融合的问题，做到按需智能化管控生产过程。

(7) 智慧炼油化工

智慧炼油化工基于以炼化企业信息系统建设与应用为核心的数字化炼油化工技术，应用AI技术在计划调度、安全环保、能源管理、装置操作、IT管控等领域实现智能化，满足生产操作优化、生产运行优化、能源管理优化和设备资产优化等降本提质增效方面的需求。

智慧生产管控一体化技术。应用VR、AR和AI等技术，横向上做到从原料运输、仓储到炼化生产、油品仓储、物料配送等环节的整个产业链的协同优化，使得生产和供应及时响应市场变化；纵向上基于分子炼油技术，做到炼厂的生产、调度、全局在线三个优化。需要进一步解决生产计划、物料供给与产品市场需求难以实现优化配置的问题，满足生产、管控和经营，以及质量、健康、安全、环保管理体系（QHSE）的溯源与监控等领域智能优化的需要，提升炼厂生产效率、最大化经营效益。

智慧设备安全监测与控制技术。通过过程装备的自我感知、自动辨识、自动预测、自适应调整、故障自愈化等技术，实现设计、制造、运行、维修等设备全生命周期智能化监测与控制。需要解决炼化设备的安全智能可控及低碳清洁运行能力不足等问题，满足设备监测预警智能化、故障诊断可视化、监控信息网络化等需要，实现炼化装备及仪器的全面智能化管控。

（8）智慧油品销售

智慧油品销售基于数字化油品销售技术，利用云计算、大数据、物联网、移动通信、AI 等新技术打通油品销售业务流程，提升油品销售数据的集中管理和大数据分析能力，形成统一的油品零售业务管理平台及技术体系。着力建立加油站物联网建设标准、视频数据采集标准，形成全面感知的信息汇聚能力，满足大数据、AI 技术与油品销售业务的深度融合需求推动创新客户体验式服务，实现车牌智能识别、客户无感支付、便利店数字营销，营造"人、车、生活"的多元经营生态圈。

线上交易平台技术。利用区块链、深度学习等技术，通过大数据对客户、产业、市场、环境的深度洞察，建立行业联盟服务标准，构建以汽服产业链为主线，汇集、赋能产业链发展的服务机构，扩展线上网络服务能力，从加油服务向用车服务、生活服务生态延伸，缔造"人、车、生活"生态圈，推动绿色能源产业服务生态建设。

智慧加油站技术。以线下加油站为核心，通过线上交易平台的客户吸引与引导，围绕车主加油服务的各类场景，基于物联网、AI 等技术和智能终端，通过智能广播、车辆自动识别、加油机器人、智能客户识别、无感支付、自动补货等技术，实现油品、非油品现场智能化服务，为客户带来更多元的服务和更好的服务体验。

（9）智慧煤炭地质勘探

智慧煤炭地质勘探通过打造天空、地面、井孔、地下、采煤工作面、长钻孔等多方位、立体式综合勘探理论及技术手段，实现对 1000 米以深煤炭资源储量及开采条件的综合精细评价，进行地面钻探、物探、化探、遥感，以及井下各类勘探成果等空间大数据的集成和融合，满足煤炭开采过程的动态探测和实时监测预警，适应无人开采或智能开采的地质保障需求。

智慧煤炭地质遥感技术。融合数字化和智能化数据传输、处理等技术，利用5G海量数据低时延传输特点，将遥感影像数据应用模式从事后处理分发向在轨处理实时传输转变，缩短从目标图像拍摄到情报信息提取的时间，提高煤炭探测及开采动态监测的准确性和实时性。需要解决数字化煤炭地质遥感技术数据传输及处理效率低、信息接收滞后、处理结果精度不够等问题，可在煤炭探测、环境监测、地质灾害监测等领域推广应用。

高速无线数据传输航空电磁技术。基于5G技术多天线收发、大数据吞吐率高等特点，将数字化航空电磁法技术从探测后数据处理转化成实时数据处理的一种更加智能的电磁探测技术，拥有快速探测、高速传输、实时监测等优势。需要解决数据传输、人机交互等低空信息网络难题，实时提供深部煤炭地质信息，实现快速探测的同时进行实时数据传输和处理。

（10）智慧煤炭开发

智慧煤炭开发通过建设以采掘生产为核心，融人员、设备、环境为一体的智能化煤矿，实现不同地质条件的智能综采和快速掘进、智能主运输和连续化辅助运输、智能供配电、安全生产监测监控、矿井综合管控和大数据分析等。

煤矿井巷全断面智能快速掘进技术。针对特大型矿井竖井、斜井和巷道的快速非爆破建设，研制煤矿防爆型竖井掘进机、竖井钻机、全断面岩巷掘进机与后配套运输及支护装备，形成井巷结构设计方法和技术标准体系，开发远程可视化掘锚支监控平台，满足掘进直径5.0-10.0米竖井、斜井、巷道需求，综合掘进速度达到200-300米/月、作业人员减少40%的目标，构建煤矿硬岩井巷智能快速掘进示范工程。

智慧开采技术。建立和完善满足智能化煤矿发展需要的信息数据库，规范信息采集中的数据校验、数据缓存、数据接口等，逐步形成全矿井全息泛化的高精度智能感知场；构建开放、安全、数据易于获取和处理的智能化煤矿大数据共享与应用平台，满足对煤矿底层子系统、传感器、智能设备等数据信息的无缝接入与深度融合处理，同时为上层应用业务模块提供数据共享与系统联动控制支撑；通过构建实时、透明、清晰的矿山采、掘、机、运、通等全系景象平台，实现对智慧煤矿各子系统的集成操控。需要解决煤矿智能化开采中的大数据同步传输、远程实时控制和多传感器集中接入等难题，以高效挖掘和利用数据，综合智能优化决策，实现煤炭智能化开采各系统的协调高效运行。

（11）煤炭低碳转化

低阶煤大型分质分级转化技术。重点研究原煤多尺度精细化深度分离与高效提质基础理论，研发低阶煤大型分质分级转化技术及装备，完善中/低温煤焦油全馏分加氢多产中间馏分油、中低温煤焦油制取轻质化燃料工艺，以及煤气无变换提浓制氢、煤化工多联产废水分质利用处理、煤焦油加氢废气回收利用等关键技术，建成 200 万吨级兰炭示范厂和千万吨级粉煤热解低阶煤（富油长焰煤）煤炭分质利用工业化示范工程。

煤炭液化及高端化工品制备技术。完善日投煤量 3000-4000 吨/日的大型高效气化炉和大型高效空分装置、大型甲醇合成塔、甲烷化反应器、大型高压压缩机等关键技术和装备，推动建设百万吨级及以上煤炭间接液化及高端化工产品（如 α-烯烃、高档润滑油、茂金属聚乙烯等）工业化生产示范工程。

（12）综合能源技术

综合能源技术基于风光储一体化、分布式多联供、相变储能等技术，结合建模仿真、协同规划、运行控制和运行维护，实现多种能源联合生产、相互转换、多形式存储、多环节协同，满足多种终端能源需求。需要进一步解决不同能源品种生产、转换、协同控制等问题，可适用于综合能源系统各环节的不同场景。

风光储一体化技术。以风力发电、太阳能发电、储能等为主要能源设施，通过多设施协同运行，形成平稳、灵活性电源，辅助送出、消纳更多风光资源，提高发电系统综合效率。主要形式包括电源侧风光储一体化、用户侧风光储一体化等，可根据发电计划、负荷预测、出力预测等，对风力发电、太阳能发电、储能系统进行协同控制与智能优化，具有提高出力曲线准确度、平滑可再生能源出力、提高电能质量等特点。需要进一步解决可再生能源发电不稳定和新能源发电计划跟踪等问题，可应用于融合高比例可再生能源的综合能源发电侧、用户侧、光储充一体化充电站等场景。

分布式多联供技术。综合利用天然气、可再生能源等清洁能源，满足用户电、热、冷、蒸汽、生活热水等多种用能需求，有效实现能源梯级利用，能源综合利用效率可达70%-90%，具有分布式供应、清洁环保、较高效率、独立运行、模块化建设等特点。需要进一步解决分布式能源的相互转换、高效利用、多能协同耦合等问题，将利用先进的信息通信技术，实现能源站的数字孪生，适用于具有电、热、冷等需求的区域用户，如商务中心、学校、医院、居民区等场景。

相变储能技术。以相变储能材料为基础的高新储能方式，利用物质在凝固/熔化、凝结/气化、凝华/升华，以及其他形式的相变过程中，吸收或放出相变潜热的原理来进行能量储存，可分为固-液相变、液-气相变和固-气相变等，具有温度恒定、蓄热密度大等特点。需要进一步解决热量供给不连续或供给与需求不协调等问题，可应用在太阳能光热利用、电供暖、废热和余热的回收利用及工业与民用建筑和空调的节能等场景。

综合能源建模仿真技术。利用系统性仿真分析方法对综合能源的运行机理、动态特性、故障场景等进行分析，包括综合能源站和能源传输网络的建模仿真，为综合能源系统规划设计、调度运行提供理论依据。在时间、空间、行为等方面具有较高的复杂性，需要进一步解决综合能源系统动态特性分析、运行模拟等问题，可应用于综合能源系统规划设计和调度运行，通过仿真结果指导系统规划的设备配置、运行过程的预判等，为系统规划设计与调度运行提供必要手段。

综合能源协同规划技术。通过科学选择各种分布式能源类型、技术路线，优化配置各种能源基础设施、设备容量、系统拓扑结构，综合设计商业模式，满足用户电、热、冷、气等多种用能需求，达到安全、高效、经济、环保等目标。具有多输入参数、多约束条件、多优化目标、多技术路线等特点，需要解决单一能源规划方法难以全方位、多角度优化多能源耦合规划设计等问题，可适用于工业、建筑、交通等各类综合能源系统。

综合能源运行控制技术。通过智能传感、通信、控制与智慧平台等技术，采用负荷预测技术与建模仿真技术对系统安全、经济运行状态进行判断，经对系统发布操作指令进行调整，实现系统电、热、冷等多种能源供需平衡。控制的对象包括综合能源各类设备的启停、出力和各类负荷的接入、大小等，需要解决区域内多种能源供需平衡、多时间尺度或多维度平衡调度等问题，可适用于含分布式多联供、光伏、储能和充电设施等较复杂的综合能源运行场景。

综合能源运行维护技术。基于 AI、大数据、云平台等技术，通过将现场运行维护人员的知识和运维经验等建立知识图谱库，根据运维具体实际情况开发成一系列的系统工具，结合无人机、机器人等设备支撑综合能源系统智慧检修、巡检、管理等业务，包括安全评估、故障诊断、智能巡检、设备健康度分析等功能。具有管理设备类型多、涉及专业类型多、应对运行工况复杂等特点，需要进一步解决综合能源运行状态复杂、设备优化运行难度大、故障及时准确预测预警等问题，可适用于工业园区、建筑和交通综合用能等场景。

中英文专业术语对照索引

结　束　语

中国已踏上全面建设社会主义现代化国家的新征程。立足新发展阶段，贯彻新发展理念，中国各行各业都必须更加突出创新发展、协调发展、绿色发展、开放发展，从而推动以人民为中心的共享发展。面对百年未有之大变局，在实现中华民族伟大复兴的战略全局中，数字化、低碳化是最具根本性和革命性的力量！中国的现代化，需要现代能源体系的支撑，这个能源体系必须是绿色低碳、智慧高效、经济安全的，必须能够支撑中国"3060"碳达峰、碳中和的战略目标。

中国在尚未完成工业化、未实现现代化的阶段主动实现碳达峰、着眼碳中和，这是人类历史上前所未有的，既无国际经验可以借鉴，也无自身经历可以复盘，必将面临非常严峻的挑战。为此，要在数字化、低碳化的大潮下推进中国的能源技术革命，打破常规和惯性，通过理论突破、技术突破、应用突破和产业边界突破，深化能源和科技领域体制机制改革，统筹规划、高效建设、科学运营、数据使"能"，实现能源行业和企业"对象、过程、规则"数字化，推动数字产业化、产业数字化。创新能源科技支持政策，着力推动新一代信息技术和数字技术与能源清洁高效开发利用技术的融合创新，为向纵深推进能源技术革命铺设一条数字之路。

为深入探索中国能源技术革命道路，《中国能源革命进展报告——能源技术革命（2021）》介绍了自 2014 年以来中国能源技术革命的进展和成效，系统梳理了能源技术革命向低碳化、数字化、智慧化发展的一系列技术和方向，以及已解决和未来需要攻克的百余个科学问题，希望为中国能源技术革命的实践提供有价值的参考。期待本报告的发布进一步激发社会各界为能源科技创新发展出谋出力的积极性。在此，我们诚挚地感谢各相关部门、研究机构、高等院校、行业学会、企业、国际机构，以及众多专家的大力支持和帮助。感谢冶金工业出版社等对报告校核、英文翻译、印刷出版等工作的大力支持。

特别要感谢以下院士在百忙之中对本报告编写工作的精心指导和无私奉献（按姓氏笔画排序）：

马永生　于俊崇　毛景文　多　吉　刘　合　江　亿

汤广福　杜祥琬　李　阳　李根生　邹才能　宋永华

武　强　金之钧　周孝信　郝　芳　郝吉明　贺克斌

贾承造　高德利　郭旭升　康红普　韩英铎　谢和平

感谢以下专家对本报告提出修改建议，以及在成稿过程中作出的贡献：

康重庆　成　钢　危　峰　王　慷　徐　洁　孟凡达

吕　发　杨洪润

Progress Report on China's Energy Revolution

Energy Technology Revolution

(2021)

Institute for Resource and Environmental Policy Studies
Development Research Center of the State Council of China

Beijing
Metallurgical Industry Press
2021

Progress Report on China's Energy Revolution
Energy Technology Revolution (2021)
Editorial Board

Huawei Technologies Co., Ltd.

Energy Research Institute, Peking University

China University of Petroleum (East China Campus)

Translators:

SONG Yunfeng   LEI Ruowei

Preface

Since President Xi Jinping proposed the promotion of energy consumption, supply, technology and system revolution as well as a new strategy of energy security to fully enhance international cooperation in 2014, China has deepened its system reform, strengthened science and technology innovation, having achieved great achievements in the establishment of a clean, low-carbon, safe, and efficient modern energy system. The energy technology innovation plays a decisive role in the energy revolution; China consistently carries out the new development concept of innovation, coordination, green, open, and sharing, having made and implemented the action plan of energy technology revolution to promote energy science and technology development, energy technology innovation, and energy industry's upgrading, which have led great progresses from theory to practice.

The theories on China's energy technology revolution have embraced a new realm. The important exposition of President Xi Jinping on energy revolution has pointed out a new direction for energy development theories with Chinese characteristics. During the 13th Five-Year Plan period, the technology innovation had driven forward the green low-carbon energy development, and fully promoted the establishment of a new energy system—being clean and low-carbon, intelligent and highly efficient, economic and secure. In May 2021, when attending the 10th National Congress of China Association for Science and Technology, President Xi declared that China would persistently put technological innovation at the core of China's national development to achieve a leapfrog development in major fields of science and technology, push forward self-reliance in key and core technologies, and strengthen the integration between innovation chains and industrial chains. The key science and technology programs should be problem-solving-oriented, focusing on the most urgent issues; we shall be sparing no efforts in overcoming difficulties and seeking for breakthroughs in the key and core technologies in oil and gas, wind power, solar power, hydro power and nuclear power. Efforts should be made in integrated innovation of new generation information technologies with the exploration and application technologies of high-efficiency clean energy, as well as in development of smart energy technologies, and fostering new sources of growth through industrial upgrading in energy technologies and their associated industries.

China's energy technology revolution practice has achieved new progresses. Since 2014, China has been steadily pushing forward the new energy security strategy of "four revolutions and one cooperation"; its energy technology level and capacity has been built up and strengthened with the energy revolution; China is leading the world in many independently developed key energy technologies. The technological progress has become the essential force to drive the energy sector's development and innovation. In coal mining, China has made progresses in green and highly-efficient mining technologies with the application rate of large scale coal mining machinery being as high as 98%; it has mastered the industrialized technologies in coal liquefaction, and the innovation in methanol to olefin technology has boosted the rapid development of the coal-to-olefins industry. In the field of oil and natural gas exploration, China's technology has advanced constantly with significant improvements in the technology and equipment on shale oil and gas survey and exploitation while China has been leading the world in the areas of highly efficient development of low permeability crude oil and heavy oil as well as new generation compound chemical flooding. In the field of electric power, China has established a complete industrial chain of clean energy generating equipment manufacturing of hydro power, wind power, solar power, nuclear power and other clean energies; the world biggest hydroelectric generating unit with capacity of 1 million kilowatt was successfully designed and built; the country is already capable of producing a full range of wind power generating units with a maximum capacity of 10 megawatt, that has continuously set the world records in new photovoltaic conversion-efficiency; it has built several nuclear power stations with advanced 3G technology having achieved break-throughs in the nuclear energy utilization technologies in the successful criticality of the high temperature gas-cooled reactor with the features of the world first 4G advanced nuclear energy system, small-scale reactors and etc. China has established the biggest, safest and most advanced power grid in the world with its power supply being the most reliable across the globe. A great number of new technologies, business models, industries such as "Internet plus" smart energy, energy storage, block chain and integrated energy services are emerging with rapid development. With the accelerated R&D, increasing maturity and wide application of the low-carbon technologies, the energy technology has become a driving force in leading the energy industry transformation, and achieving carbon peaking and neutrality.

The major changes unseen in a century has spawn transformation in world energy technologies. In recent years, traditional security issues such as geopolitical strategies, game playing among big powers, and arms races, which have been increasingly becoming the central topics in world affairs and international relations, together with global impact of the "exceptional non-traditional security" pandemic issue of Covid-19, have obviously raised the uncertainties in future international relations. In the "post-Covid-19 era", there will be significant uncertainties in the world economic growth. The drastic volatility in the global energy market will continue to exist, while the international energy structure will be experiencing deep re-adjustment. Meanwhile, energy technologies will accelerate the transformation that is conducive to both the green recovery of the world economy and combating global climate change. Green and low-carbon is also becoming the main direction of energy technology innovation with the focus on clean and highly-efficient use of the traditional fossil energy, large-scale exploration and application of new energies, safe use of nuclear power, global energy interconnection, and pilot programs & applications of large-scale energy storage. Innovation in energy technologies has entered into a dynamic era with an unprecedent fast development in new energy technologies, which will have long term critical and deep impact on the global energy pattern and the world economic development.

China's energy technology revolution faces both challenges and opportunities. With the large country strategic competition game between China and the US being increasingly intense, after playing the cards of "trade, technology and finance" to China, the US is currently playing the cards of "energy and climate change". The EU, also experiencing unprecedented challenges in pushing forward its own sustainable development and green economy recovery; the rule changing in international trade brought by the carbon border adjustment mechanism driven by Europe, the US and other advanced countries to be implemented will certainly have long term deep impact on China's participation in the international industrial chains and supply chains, which will make it even more obvious for China to tackle the weak links in the basic theories in energy technologies. China is encountered with an increasingly prominent issue of "bottlenecking" technologies and obstacles of establishing its own system of low-carbon energy technologies. In view of the huge challenges brought by the major changes unseen in a century in the world, China will go all out to cultivate new opportunities in the times of crisis and will open a new front in the changing situation, especially in improving the overall efficiency of the energy innovation system with the advantage of China's a new system concentrating nationwide effort and resources on key national undertakings. This will gradually mitigate China's dependence on foreign technologies, while enabling technology innovation to be the strong support for China to achieve its strategic goals of realizing carbon peaking in 2030 and carbon neutrality in 2060 (abbreviated as "3060" goals).

Technology determines the future of energy and it creates the energy of the future. Both the rapid development of the non-fossil energy and the clean use of the fossil energy, will increasingly depend on the drive of crossover innovations in science and technology. The energy sector of China is evolving to be highly digitalized and low-carbon. Newly emerging technologies such as 5G, Internet of Things, AI, block chain, cloud, big data, edge computing will integrate further with the new energy sector, paving a digitalized path in achieving China's energy revolution and its strategic goals of "3060". Based on these reasons, Development Research Center of the State Council has commissioned senior specialists and scholars in the energy sector to compile this report under the guidance of a series of important speeches, instructions and comments made by President Xi Jinping. The report sums up systematically the practice and exploration in China's energy technology revolution conducted in and by various departments, regions, research institutions, colleges and universities, industrial associations, key enterprises since the strategic thought on China's energy revolution was promulgated. It focuses on new development stage, analyzes low-carbon transformation of the energy sector as well as the urgent science issues and technological "bottlenecks" to solve. The report also projects the global and China's directions and prospects of the energy technology revolution and the key digital technologies in the future decade to better serve China's "3060" goals, to continuously push forward China's long term and in-depth energy technology revolution, and to provide strong support for China's 2030 goal of carbon peaking and for the new plans of the energy industry in the 14th Five-Year Plan period.

Contents

I. Prominent Achievements of the Energy Technology Revolution during the 13th Five-Year Plan Period

During the 13th Five-Year Plan period, China has implemented the innovation-oriented development strategy in depth, constructed a green, low-carbon and smart energy technology innovation system, and further improved its energy technologies and energy industry related equipment. China has taken great efforts in the integration of energy technology with new-generation information technology as well as advanced manufacturing technology, exploring new paths in innovating energy production and consumption with the support of the development of Internet plus smart energy. China has quickened its new types of renewable energy technology innovation including wind power, and photovoltaic innovation to support China's renewable energy sector to be changed from being a leader in the industry to being a leader in the respect of technology; the digital photovoltaic innovation promoted the integration of photovoltaic power generation with agriculture, fishery, and construction technologies to create new space of complementary applications areas in these industries. China has accelerated the development of the hydrogen energy industrial chain technology and equipment for green hydrogen production, energy storage and application. Furthermore, it has greatly boosted the expansion of the industrial chain for hydrogen fuel-cell vehicles (HFCV). China has also supported R&D, and application in energy storage technology and equipment for all links and occasions of all energy resources with key efforts having been taken in pushing forward the complementary development between energy storage and renewable energy sources. Guided and led by the pilot programs and projects, new technologies, new models, new situations of businesses have been continuously emerging and have resulted in the "multiplier effect" in China's energy innovation and development, which has laid a solid technological foundation for carbon peaking before 2030.

i. Fossil Energy Resources Sector Technology

During the 13th Five-Year Plan period, with the objective to help establish a clean, low-carbon, smart and efficient, economically safe system in the field of fossil fuels, based on its own needs at the new development stage and following the global trends in technology development, China has carried forward the upgrading of digitization, overcome the key technological problems restraining the development of the energy industry, and formed a series of internationally advanced technologies to provide powerful support for the security of coal, oil and natural gas supply.

1. Coal

During the 13th Five-Year Plan period, China has substantially enhanced its independent innovation ability of the coal industry, having established a science and technology innovation system with enterprises as the main entities, the market as the guide, and collaboration among industries, universities and research institutes, primarily formed an industrial research and development platform and a rational distribution of innovation bases featuring complementary functions and clear guidance and realized the transformation of the coal technology from only tracking and following others' development to surpassing and leading the world in certain aspects. Currently, China has basically established a coal mining geological security system focusing on safety and high efficiency; the technologies and equipment of trough wave seismic, radio wave perspective detection technology, directional long drill drilling, broken soft coal seam gas directional drilling have reached the international leading position; the technologies of three-dimensional seismic exploration, DC method, transient electromagnetic, geological radar and others have been widely applied. The comprehensive technological system of safety, efficiency and green mining, has been established. A fast tunneling system with tunneling anchor unit, self-mobile machine tail, and anchor transport machine has been development, forming various subsidence technologies such as solid filling, paste filling, high hydro material filling and other subsidence technologies; 8.8 meter ultra-high surface mining is carried out, having proposed the "unmanned operation, manual-patrol" intelligent mining production mode. The clean coal technology system including coal processing, application, conversion, and pollution control is improved. Measurements and calculations show that the carbon emission per ton of coal produced at technologically advanced facilities is 50% lower than the rest, thus effectively reducing the intensity of carbon emission.

Firstly, in the respect of geological survey and exploration, China has built up a comprehensive technology system of coal resource survey that fits well the features of coal resource distribution with the "coal geological exploration" becoming "comprehensive coal resource survey and exploration" focusing on coordinated surveys including coalbed methane, shale gas, tight sandstone gas and covering coal exploration, pit construction, safe production, and environment protection. China has successfully developed geological radar equipment and methods for detecting in-depth mine disaster sources with a depth of 80 meter, 1.6 times more than the previous depth and 75% average verification rate of geological structure; the underground low frequency geological radar detection system has been designed with computed tomography imaging X-ray inversion software covering 300 meter working face with the accuracy being increased by more than 30%. Secondly, on the coal exploitation, China's coal mining machinery-making capability is among the most advanced in the world and has successfully developed a series of complete sets of equipment such as 8.8 meter full-seam-height mining equipment, 7 meter super height intelligent fully mechanized top coal caving machine, and pure water hydraulic support. Nationwide, China has built about 500 intelligent mining faces, having employed robot groups, auger anchor robots, gangue selection robots, and inspection robots in the pits, and formed four intelligent coal mining modes including intelligent unmanned operation in thin and medium thick coal seams, man-machine-ring intelligent coupling high efficiency fully mechanized mining for large mining height coal seams, intelligent control of fully mechanized caving face and man-assisted auxiliary coal caving, as well as intelligent plus mechanized operation under complex conditions. The construction of intelligent coal mining has continuously advanced changes in the ways of coal mining production, pushed on smart interconnectivity between all the links in production, and effectively reduced the number of workers in pits. By the end of 2020, Shanxi Province, by forcefully promoting intelligent coal mining, it is hoped to reduce 60% to 70% of the workers in the working faces with such intelligent coal mining system, and over 50% of the workers in the intelligent coal mines. Thirdly, in the coal chemical industry, China has made great breakthroughs in developing coal to olefin and coal to ethylene glycol technology and equipment, among which manufacturing techniques, key large-scale equipment and special catalysts' localization have been gradually realized. Large-scale coal chemical equipment for coal liquefaction and coal to olefin equipment have been developed and applied; engineering technologies for high efficiency and large-scale modern coal liquefaction and coal to olefin processes have been pioneered; the world's first direct coal liquefaction and coal to olefin project has achieved sustained and stable operation.

（1）Geological Exploration

Digital Coal Geological Remote Sensing Technology　　The monitoring system based on the high-resolution remote sensing data integrates big data transmission and processing technology with rapid capture of the target space planning pictures, combining remote sensing digital survey monitoring and application, determines position of coal series and coal seams on the surface or underground, marking their special boundaries. Digital geological remote sensing technology is featured by its extensive visibility, intelligence, high speed, and high perspective. Moreover, it is able to solve the inversion problem in remote sensing geological interpretation, and to acquire more accurate and effective geological interpretation results through parameter adjustments based on machine recognition and eliminating intervening factors affecting inversion quality. This technology has basically solved the challenges in coal resource assessment caused by multi-source heterogeneous composition problems such as massive data in earthquake and logging analysis. Currently, China has developed such technologies as airborne hyperspectral identification, aerospace high resolution equipment, and surface detection, having formed a comprehensive 3S technology application research system featured by the combination of the Global Positioning System (GPS), the Geographic Information System (GIS) and the Remote Sensing (RS), which is widely employed in the large-scale and quick scanning of the arid and semi-arid regions providing references for the dynamic monitoring of coal area survey and mining as well as for marking the post-mining goaf areas.

Digital Airborne Electromagnetic Detection Technology   This technology replaces data-driven program with object-driven program, while integrating wireless communication technology, intelligent recognition, target information extraction technology and nonlinear inversion of massive data technology to calibrate field values of the geological information through machine learning, and three-dimensional inversion geological interpretation by parallel clusters. This technology, featured by high-speed operation, strong circumstance adaptability and great volume of data collection, has essentially helped with forming a detection system characterized by combination of fixed-wing and podded electromagnetic methods supplemented by ground air electromagnetic method. This technology has solved the critical problem of noise suppression in the object-driven program; furthermore it can obtain higher signal-to-noise ratio and deeper geological information signals while raising coal resource detection capacity; it is widely used in basic geological and energy resource survey and evaluation of complex landforms and geology such as hills and plateaus.

（2）Coal Mining

Digital Fast Speed Tunneling Technology   Based on spatial multi-dimensional synchronization technology of excavation, the systematic and integrated designs for tunneling engineering are developed which has greatly improved the efficiency of tunneling and tunnel formation through synchronization of all links in the production process supported by tunneling techniques and equipment innovation. These designs have essentially solved the core technological problems in the following areas such as parallel excavation and support, full width cutting, automatic support, flexible transport, coordinated control, and smart safety check system, and realized the functions such as automatic ranging follow-up of each equipment, continuous transport, coal flow equilibrium, and cooperative motion control. At present, the newly developed modular intelligent anchor re-loader, flexible continuous transport system and other complete sets of equipment and platforms, have already been successfully applied to large coal mining areas with good geological cladding conditions, having increased the operating efficiency of equipment, improved the level of equipment safety and intelligence, achieved self-commissioning, self-organization and self-stability of the collaborative control system.

Intelligent Mining Technology   Based on the additional autonomous decision-making function in its automation system, this technology can detect the changes of the enclosing rock condition and external environment, and automatically adjust the operational parameter with its capacities of intelligent detecting, decision-making, and controlling; in this way automatic learning, autonomous decision-making and self-adapting mining are realized. After the intelligent remodeling of the 1.4 to 2.2 meter thin-to-medium seams at Huangling No.1 Mine (Shaanxi Province), only one operator is needed for the routine inspection of the work face and mining in tunnel is controlled and monitored by the above-ground control center or centralized control room in the underground tunnel, marking a major breakthrough in unmanned coal mining technology. China has overcome the technical difficulty of full-seam-height mining for the 8.2 meter seams; the first set of fully mechanized mining technology and intelligent control system for 8.2 meter seam mining in China as well as in the world was developed and successfully applied at Jinjitan Mine (Shaanxi Province); the monthly production set a record of 2.02 million tons of ROM coal, reaching the world advanced level.

（3）Clean Conversion

Thermal Power Generation Technology   This technology includes the combustion technologies focusing on boilers, as well as various kinds of pumps, feed-water heaters, steam condensers, pipelines, water-wall steam water technology, turbine generators, electric technology and control technology such as main transformers. It turns the chemical energy of coal into electric power, the main equipment of which includes subcritical coal-fired generator set, supercritical coal-fired generator unit and ultra-supercritical coal-fired generator unit. During the 13th Five-Year Plan period, China's thermal power generation technology was among the most advanced in the world, progressing persistently in the direction of high parameter, great capacity, high efficiency and low-carbon emission. The clean conversion of thermal power generation technology mainly uses four kinds of technologies to improve efficiency and reduce emissions: firstly, by replacing the small backward and high energy-consuming units with advanced high capacity and high parameter thermal power generation units, which are represented by ultra-critical and super-ultra-critical technologies; secondly, using mature coal gasification technology in coal chemical industry to integrate steam gas combined cycle technology to achieve clean and efficient power generation, represented by the Integrated Gasification Combined Cycle (IGCC); thirdly, using biomass fuel and coal mixed combustion, and using biomass instead of coal-fired and coal-powered coupling power generation, to reduce coal consumption and emissions, represented by biomass gasification and coal mixed-combustion coupling power generation technology; fourthly, the current operating power generation units' upgrading for energy saving, for ultra-low emission, for flexibility, and for optimized operation which are represented by digital coal power plants. The super-ultra-critical power generation technology has the characteristics of being reliable, large-scale, high-efficiency and clean, basically having solved the problems of improving the efficiency of coal-fired power generation and energy saving and emission reduction. China's 600,000 kilowatt super-ultra-critical coal-fired unit consumes 278 g/kWh coal, 30 g/kWh less than the coal consumption of the same capacity subcritical units, being able to save 60,000 tons of standard coal per year compared to the same capacity subcritical unit. IGCC technology has the characteristics of high power generation efficiency and good environmental protection performance, but the complex system leads to high investment cost. Biomass and coal-fired coupling power generation technology can make comprehensive use of a variety of energy sources, which can initially solve the problems of traditional energy shortage, stockpiling biomass resources in open areas, wasteful burning, pollution and carbon reduction etc. With the gradual integration between thermal power technology and information communication technology, the technological path for digital thermal power plants is increasingly mature with more reasonable economic cost and more prominent renovation effect. Digital coal power plants are constructed and managed with three-dimensional digital design and intelligent management, featuring functions such as 3D modeling, big data platform and robot inspection, which has solved the technical difficulties in improving energy efficiency, enhancing operation safety, lowering equipment operation and repairing cost, raising the peak-load regulation capability of the generating sets, and reducing pollutants and carbon emission. Up until 2020, 890 million kilowatt of coal power units in China had reached ultra-low emission levels, accounting for more than 80% of the total 1.08 billion kilowatt installed capacity of coal power, and having established the world's largest clean coal power supply system.

Chemical Engineering Technologies of Coal to Oil and Coal to Olefin China has successfully resolved a series of problems of the world such as direct coal liquefaction and coal to olefin engineering, key equipment and super-large and super-thick equipment manufacturing, stability and reliability of system integration, as well as safe, stable and sustained operation of apparatus, successfully developed and applied a complete set of independently-designed technologies of a million-ton scale direct liquefaction and 600,000 ton coal to olefin conversion, built the world's first demonstration project as well as an industrial demonstration program of indirect coal liquefaction capacity of 4 million ton, the largest production capacity for a single plant in the world. China has built the "Shenning Furnace" of its own proprietary intellectual property rights which can manufacture synthetic diesel with ultra low sulfur (ULS) (close to zero), low aromatics, low ash, and high cetane value, while its emission index in sulfur dioxide, nitrogen oxides and smoke is far below China's national standards.

2. Oil and Gas

During the 13th Five-Year Plan period, China's oil and gas industry, facing the challenge of large volatilities of the international oil prices, accelerated the transformation of its development mode, and implemented development strategies such as security, differentiation, low cost, internationalization and integration. The industry has taken great efforts in promoting high quality development, prioritizing quality and efficiency, strengthening reform and innovation, tackling key problems by taking the advantage of the new nation-wide mobilization mechanism. The sector has reached the internationally advanced level in key technologies or technical applications and development in the fields of deep oil and gas exploration and development, non-regular oil and gas exploration and development, intelligent and integrated refining and chemical plant management and control, and intelligent oil sales, providing a strong support for the oil and gas industry in green and efficient development. In 2020, China's domestic crude oil production reached 195 million tons and natural gas approximately 190 billion cubic meters. The industry's energy consumption growth rate dropped from 6.9% in the 12th Five-Year Plan period to 3% in 2020. Carbon dioxide emissions were approximately 100 million tons in oil and gas exploration and development, and about 500 million tons in the refining and chemical industry.

Firstly, in the respect of exploration and development, there have formed the fine exploration theories and evaluation reports on fault basins in east China, the theories and assessments of deep marine carbonate oil and gas formation, assessment on the patterns of different enrichment of tight clastic rocks in the central and western regions and the evaluation analysis on sweet spots, theories and exploration evaluation of marine shale gas enrichment mechanism, continental shale oil and gas occurrence mechanism and classification evaluation, passive continental margin basin oil and gas accumulation theory and deep water exploration evaluation, single-point high-density seismic and high-end imaging software platform, as well as ultra-deep exploration engineering technologies. China has also developed key technologies in ultra-deep oil and gas mining engineering, regular pressure and deep shale gas low cost development technology, heterogeneous combined flooding, enhanced oil recovery of high-sulfur gas fields, effective exploration of tight gas, ultra-deep drilling and completion. China has further developed rotation guidance instruments, high-temperature and high-voltage directional logging instruments, high-performance automated intelligent drilling rigs and fracking vehicles, new high-efficiency rock breaking tools, etc. special operation equipment, promoted the digital upgrade of exploration and development technology and equipment, and basically achieved high-quality exploration and profitable development of different types of oil and gas reservoirs. Secondly, in the respect of refining and chemical sectors, China has mastered the world's advanced full-process refining technology, covering from heavy oil deep catalytic cracking to low-carbon olefins, multi-yield isomerized alkanes catalytic deterioration process, S-Zorb gasoline adsorption desulfurization, low-pressure continuous recombination, catalytic diesel conversion and high octane gasoline production technology, to diesel ultra-deep hydrogenation desulfurization, diesel liquid phase circular hydrogenation and other technologies; China has had its own IP in the main oil and chemical technologies including full million tonnage ethylene technology, CBL-IX heavy raw material cracking furnace, large aromatics auxiliary technology, continuous re-organization technology, propylene alkylization isopropylene complete set of technology, hydrogen peroxide propylene epoxy propane complete set of technology, a new generation of high-performance styrene thermoplastic elastomer technology, ring hexone ammonia hexylamide technology, toluene methylation of xylation toluene technology, etc.; the localization of major equipment such as cracking gas compressor, C_2H_4O reactor, polyester main reactor, hydrogen cracking reactor, slag oil hydrogen reactor, million-ton compressor units has been achieved; break throughs of a number of key technologies of new chemical materials, including carbon fiber and its composite material manufacturing, ultra-high molecular high density polyethylene battery diaphragm, ultra-high-pressure polyethylene cable special materials, polypropylene infusion bag special materials, chemical fiber biodegradable materials, hydrogenated styrene thermoplastic elastomers, flame retardant acrylic fibers and so on. Thirdly, in the field of oil and gas storage and transportation, vigorous development of pipeline transportation and promotion of the layout adjustment of oil depots have driven the forming of flexible, easy and convenient, inventory and sales balance, and secured supplies; various finished oil product sales channels have been set up in the southwest, Yantaiwen, Shaoxing-Hangzhou, Zhanjiang and finished oil product warehouses in Changxindian, Beijing. Fourthly, on oil product sales, a network of business systems based on its distribution channels has been set up with the geographical restrictions being gradually eliminated and a national sales network of refined oil basically has come into being. China has initially developed and began to apply the large-scale multi-layer distribution management information system of gas stations with special features of refined oil sales, successfully established the world's largest refined oil sales management information technology clusters, innovated technologies of distinct Chinese characteristics of fuel dispensers, metering and pricing, gas cards, and forecourts of gas stations, gradually introduced Internet payment and marketing tools to address the newly emerged requirements from consumers which have been promoted to large enterprises, so to effectively support the standardized and intensive development of large sales networks of refined oil.

（1）Exploration and Development

Digital Oil and Gas Exploration Technology   This informatized exploration technology system is based on tools of geology, geophysical prospecting（including seismic exploration and gravity, magnetic, electrical, and chemical prospecting), and geophysical logging, etc. taking advantage of the integration of the new generation information technologies including three-dimensional visualization and big data management platform. This technology helps solve problems in oil and gas resource evaluation, reservoir prediction and lithology identification caused by the multi-source, heterogeneous, and large volume of digital content resources acquired by exploration technology, so as to meet the digitized needs of reservoir evaluation, identification and parameter prediction, etc., to achieve accurate and efficient reservoir prediction, reservoir evaluation and description.

Digital Oil and Gas Development Technology   Based on the theory of seepage mechanics combined with the actual condition of reservoir physics, this technology helps analyze the regularities of reservoir and fluid seepage, construct digital oil and gas reservoirs, having achieved a dynamic simulation of real time oil reservoirs and the perception, analysis, prediction, optimization and decision-making of the production environment in the virtual environment. The technology initially provides solutions to the problems in production scheme's decision-making, production forecasting model, work flow simulation, and integration of oil and gas ground engineering construction and oil production engineering. It can basically meet the needs in real-time control of oil and gas development, production measure optimization, station equipment safety and digitized metering and safe operation.

Digital Oil and Gas Well Formation Technology An information-based drilling and completion technology system is established based on automated drilling rigs, downhole high-precision measurement instruments, visualization equipment, fine drilling and completion design, with real-time data transmission near the drill bit, and taking advantage of digital platform and remote decision support center. This technology basically provides solutions to problems in target identification, trajectory optimization, speed and efficiency improvement in complex formations. It can initially meet the engineering requirements in accurate downhole measurement and control, timely and accurate prediction of complex conditions and accidents, dynamic optimization of drilling parameters, as well as online early warning and diagnosis of equipment.

（2）Oil Refining and Chemicals

Integrated Technology of Digital Production Management and Control With the application of the technologies of data acquisition, process control and production optimization analysis of refining and chemical production units, through digital modeling, simulation and optimization of process flow, as well as production management and product marketing, the technology system of a digital chemical plant has been set up integrating virtual and real physical plant. It basically has solved the problems in refining and chemical production process control caused by the complexity of production raw materials, process flow and production control, as well as the large variety of products and the great impact of market prices. It can meet the requirements for the coordinated operation of crude oil (material) and energy supply in refineries, as well as the digital integration of the whole business chain of product storage, transportation, marketing services and production management.

Safety Monitoring and Control Technology for Digital Equipment With the application of technologies for digital monitoring & control, equipment real-time prediction, and digital risk management, the following functions are achieved: equipment status identification and prediction, adaptable adjustment in the control of external environmental disturbance or self-error and autonomous maintenance support for decision-making. This technology provides initial solutions for equipment reliability and stability in the full life cycle of the refinery's production process, and can meet the needs of safe and reliable production and operation of the refinery and the harmonious coexistence of human, machine and environment.

（3）Oil Sales

The Technology of Online Trading Platform   Thanks to the introduction of the new technologies and concepts of the Internet, and through the establishment of a business service center and the comprehensive storage and utilization of data, as well as through outsourcing, price negotiation, sales and distribution, China has forged the full process online transaction technology that can achieve online ordering of oil products, product management, price management, marketing management, logistics tracking, and customer evaluation etc. It provides initial solutions to the challenges such as fast customer connection, fast oil sales, accurate and rapid settlement; it can also improve the Internet service capacity of "customer-focused" sellers of refined-oil.

The Technology of Digital Gas Station   Based on technologies such as smart card and data warehouse, China has built a technical system in retail management covering refined oil procurement, sales, inventory, quantity and price. It basically solves the multi-level management problem of large oil companies in the respect of large number of gas stations, long supply chain, and over extensive networks; it can help with providing accurate collection and timely understanding of the network production and operation data of different gas stations, so as to provide secured management services for large fleets of oil vehicles in their refueling and payment; it has supported with meeting the requirements of refined-oil sellers for their internal management and operational risk prevention and control.

（4）Natural Gas Power Generation

Natural gas power generation technologies include those related with gas turbine, steam turbine, generator, heat exchanger and pump. The main equipment includes integrated gas-steam circular unit and natural gas distributed multi-cogeneration unit. At present in China, in gas-steam integrated circular units, mostly 9E, 9F and other large gas turbines are applied with much higher power generation efficiency, improved start-up time, lower emissions and higher flexibility. With the application of natural gas distributed multi cogeneration technology, power is generated through thermal power units such as gas turbine, gas internal combustion engine and micro gas turbine; the high-temperature flue gas and cooling water generated are used to supply cooling and heating through the secondary heat utilization unit, so to meet the energy requirements of electricity, heating and cooling. The natural gas power generation have significant advantages over thermal power generation in terms of the emissions of various pollutants and carbon. The carbon dioxide emission per kilowatt hour of 9HA gas power plant (313g) is much lower—over 50% lower than that of thermal power plant; the nitrogen oxide emission per kilowatt hour (0.07g) is about 0.1g lower than that of 660 megawatt thermal plant; the emission of sulfide and soot is close to zero.

ii. Non-fossil Fuel Energy Sector's Technology

By 2020, China's installed capacity of non-fossilfuel energy power generation was 950 million kilowatt, accounting for 43% of the total national installed capacity, including 280 million kilowatt of wind power, 250 million kilowatt of photovoltaic power generation, 370 million kilowatt of hydropower and 50 million kilowatt of nuclear power.[1] With the rapid development of non-fossil energy power generation technology, the industrial chain of equipment manufacturing has been established. While the installed capacity and power generation of non-fossil energy maintain a high growth rate, the power deprecation and deprecation rate are reduced respectively compared with 2015, achieving "dual rise and dual fall". Through optimization of energy structure and improvement of energy efficiency, the CO_2 emission intensity per unit power generation is reduced by about 10% compared with that of 2015.

1. Wind Energy

Wind power generation technology refers to the technology that converts wind energy into mechanical energy through the application of blades and transmission system of wind turbine; mechanical energy is then converted into electric energy by generator. China started the development of large scale wind power in 2005. By 2010, the accumulative installed capacity of wind power had been ranked world No.1 Until now, China has maintained its world No.1 position. The annual newly installed capacity in China has remained at the scale of 10 million kilowatt. China's wind power equipment manufacturing industry has also been changed from being a follower to a leader in the world in many respects. According to the

---

[1]　Data source: list of national power industry statistical express in 2020.

applications, wind power technology can be divided into onshore centralized wind power, onshore decentralized wind power and offshore wind power.

Technology of Onshore Wind Power Generation   Technologies in this aspect include those of design, R&D and construction of up to 156 meter diameter wind turbine, 4-8 megawatt or even 10 megawatt and above fan model, and unit of minimum wind speed of 4. 5m/s; the technologies also include a series of technical systems such as blades, gearbox, generator and electric control system. China's onshore wind power technologies and equipment manufacturing capacity have reached world-class level; the wind turbine technology has the trend of development towards being large-scale, intelligent, efficient and highly reliable. The power capacity of wind turbines has been continuously improved. At present, the maximum single unit capacity of onshore wind power hoisting in China is 10 megawatt; the power generation capacity of fans is more than twice that of fans with the same capacity 10 years ago; and the continuous innovation of low wind speed and high tower technology has greatly improved the economical upside of onshore wind energy resources.

Distributed Wind Power Technology   Distributed wind power technology has the characteristics of small scale, low access voltage level and easily connectable to the local power grid nearby for consumption. In view of the shortage of land resources and proximity to residents, a series of technical systems with strong adaptability have been developed, such as basic deep burial technology, anti-corrosion technology and noise reduction technology. Distributed wind power technology can be applied to industrial parks, field ridges, and artificial reefs.

Offshore Wind Power Technology   It covers a series of technical systems, such as the models of 6 megawatt to 14 megawatt and above, single base, jacket base, ice resistance, flexible DC transmission, design and R&D of large-scale wind power stations in sea areas that are far away from the coast. China's design capacity of offshore wind turbine foundation has been continuously improved; great progresses have been made in the transportation, installation and construction technologies, breakthroughs accomplished in the manufacturing of main equipment parts and key technologies, which are on par with those internationally advanced ones.

Digital Wind Power Technology   Based on big data and Internet, and with the application of new sensing technologies such as wind power radar, enhanced pneumatic technology, wind power prediction, fault prediction, life analysis and other system technologies, China has developed a series of technical systems such as intelligent wind farm design, accurate site selection, fan selection, intelligent control, wind farm operation optimization and adjustment support system. Through the intelligent upgrading of wind farm and wind turbine, this kind of technology can effectively improve the output of wind turbine, reduce the failure rate, reduce operation & maintenance cost of wind farm and wind turbine; it can also reduce the hourly power cost of wind power.

2. Solar Power

Photovoltaic Power Generation Technology　It consists of technical systems based on established equipment and technologies such as solar cell array, battery pack, charge/discharge controller, inverter, AC distribution cabinet, solar tracking control system. At present, the industrialization technology of China is at the world advanced level; the planning of the overall national layout of cutting-edge technologies has been accelerated, while the manufacturing of main equipment has been localized. China's newly added photovoltaic installed capacity has been ranked world No.1 for many consecutive years since 2013; the cumulative installed capacity since 2015 and the industrial scale since 2007 have also been ranked world No.1. In 2020, China set a record of the highest efficiency of solar cells in the world for four times, while the average conversion efficiency of mainstream photovoltaic modules in the new photovoltaic market reached over 20%.

Solar Thermal Power Generation Technology　With this kind of technology, large scale array parabolic or disc mirror is used to collect solar heat energy; the steam is provided through heat exchange device, while power generation is accomplished in combination with the process of traditional steam turbine generator. At present, it mainly includes four types of technologies: tower, slot, butterfly and Fresnel. The products of domestic manufacturers of solar thermal power generation equipment are listed in six categories: solar concentration, heat absorption, heat transfer/storage & the materials, steam turbine generator units, integrated control systems and auxiliary systems; they basically have covered the full industrial chain of solar thermal power generation. By 2020, the cumulative installed capacity of solar thermal power generation in China was about 450,000 kilowatt.

Digital Photovoltaic Power Station Technology　It is a technical system composed of digital technology and prediction covering all links of photovoltaic planning, construction, operation control and operation maintenance. It has the characteristics of real-time collection of operation monitoring data, remote monitoring, remote automatic operation and maintenance, automatic cleaning, remote fault diagnosis and rapid processing. This technology basically solves the fine management problem of the smallest unit of the photovoltaic power station, improves the power generation efficiency of the photovoltaic system, and enhances the sensing capacity of the fluctuation of photovoltaic output in real time, while providing safety and stability, intelligent operation and maintenance; it can also help reduce labor cost, as well as enhance the early warning capacity and risk prevention for the operation & maintenance of the power station. The technology can be applied to centralized photovoltaic power stations, photovoltaic in buildings, pavement photovoltaic, photovoltaic corridors and photovoltaic landscapes. From regular maintenance to condition-based maintenance, from passive inspection to active inspection, this technology has supported remote operation and maintenance with fewer people, so as to achieve "no-operator" or "fewer operator" operation and maintenance.

3. Hydropower

The optimization of China's hydropower structure has been accelerated, with the construction of export channels being carried out extensively, the technologies and equipment in this sector steadily improved, and the full industrial chain's "overseas development" accelerated. During the 13th Five-Year Plan period, about 30 million kilowatt of large-scale conventional hydropower projects were approved to be constructed. With the commencement of large-scale hydropower and water conservancy projects such as Baihetan on Jinsha River, the development layout of large hydropower bases in the upper reaches of the Yellow River, Wujiang River, Hongshui River, Yalong River, Dadu River and Jinsha River has been basically completed; small hydropower technologies with an installed capacity of 25 megawatt and below have gradually been phased out.

Large Hydropower Generation Technology   It covers a series of technical systems, including technologies of water resources evaluation, hydropower development, hydraulic structure engineering, hydropower station equipment design, installation/operation/ maintenance, and hydropower station operation. It converts the gravitational potential energy and kinetic energy of water into mechanical energy; with turbine driving the generator to rotate, the mechanical energy is converted eventually into electrical energy. During the 13th Five-Year Plan period, China made breakthroughs in key technologies and related scientific development of large-scale hydropower, such as the successful development and commencement of operation of the world's largest hydropower unit with a maxim single unit capacity of 1 million kilowatt, the design of 300 meter high dam, the design of super large underground powerhouse, the analysis of the transition process of complex water conveyance system, and the structural design of large water conveyance system. Now China has become the "leader" of hydropower in the world after catching up with advanced countries.

Intelligent Hydropower Station Technology   Based on the operation status data obtained by intelligent sensors, a new generation of information technology is applied to form a technical system with the characteristics of informatization and digital simulation calculation, online construction management, online control and early warning; it can monitor the production site, predict and diagnose accidents, provide real-time motor status information, and realize the integration of hydropower station construction, operation, management and regulation, achieve centralized operation, maintenance and monitoring of multiple hydropower stations to improve safety, to reduce the number of operators and to achieve fully automatic unmanned dam operation. This technology basically provides solutions of real-time dynamic analysis and coupling simulation prediction of geological environment, structures, management program and scheduling in hydropower project construction. It can ensure dam safety, timely and accurate collection of data, formulation of power generation plan, improvement of power generation controllability while reducing work force, manual intervention, and operation cost.

4. Nuclear Energy

The application of nuclear energy technology is the most typical application in the civil field. With over 13 years of hard efforts, China has developed from zero technology with weak technical capacity to be a strong player to be able to design, build, operate and maintain the most advanced 4G nuclear power station, to be the first to implement the 4G nuclear power generation technology, and with many significant breakthroughs being made in a number of nuclear energy utilization technologies including the new generation of nuclear power plants and small reactors. By 2020, the installed capacity of nuclear power generation in operation was about 50 million kilowatt and the installed capacity is about 10 million kilowatt.

Advanced 3G and 4G Nuclear Power Technology　China has independently developed "Hualong-1" and "Guohe-1" 3G nuclear power plants at megawatt level; their main technical and safety performance indicators have already reached the world advanced level. The characteristics of this technology mainly include higher usability and longer service life for the reactor, and lower serious accident rate and core loss frequency rate, with application of active and non-active safety technology, making interference unnecessary within 72 hours of the taking place of accidents, further improving the safety of nuclear power generation. At present, China's nuclear power generation sector has formed a relatively complete industrial system, with an independent and complete manufacturing capacity of about 8-10 sets/year. Major equipment and key materials such as main pump, pressure vessels, components in the reactor, fuel components, steam generators, Digital Instrument & Control System (DCS), super large castings and forgings have been localized, and the localization rate has reached over 85%. In Sept 2021, breakthrough was made in the construction of high temperature gas cooling reactor with 4G nuclear power generation technology; the pilot project of high temperature gas cooling reactor nuclear power station in Shidao Bay gradually reached nearly, and the for the first time, reached criticality. The generation units officially have entered "continuous nuclear reactor" status. In the first world modular high temperature gas cooling reactor power station, the localization rate of the equipment used in the pilot project reached 93.4%, symbolizing China has been changed from a follower to a leader in the advance nuclear energy technology field.

Small Nuclear Reactor Technology Due to the differences in application purpose, there are many kinds of small reactors. The small nuclear reactor technology represented by "Linglong-1" has achieved breakthroughs The output power of a single unit is less than 300,000 kilowatt; it has the technical characteristics of miniaturization, modularization and integration. The technology has high safety standard, good flexibility and extensive applications. It can be directly applied in industrial areas and densely populated areas as a distributed power supply to provide urban/regional power supply, civil heating and industrial process heating, or marine resource development and seawater de-salination.

Digital Reactor Technology It is a comprehensive technology based on the development of reactor basic theory, numerical calculation technology and computer technology at specific stage; it is also known as virtual reactor or numerical reactor. In the super large-scale and high-performance computing system, the technology uses computing software and various databases to integrate numerical simulation to simulate various characteristics of reactor life cycle. Through the development of high-precision design analysis program and the improvement of analysis methods, it can accurately analyze the transient response characteristics of reactor core and system; it can also provide accurate understanding of the conservative margin of major safety and thermal limit parameters such as critical heat flux and cladding peak temperature; it can support the improvement of overall performance parameters such as reactor rated power. Digital reactor can help improve the power capacity, burnup rate, life cycle and economy of nuclear power plants.

iii. Energy Infrastructure and Demand Side Energy Conservation and Carbon Reduction Technology

During the 13th Five-Year Plan period, under the guidance of the new energy security strategy, China implemented the national basic policy of carrying out resources conservation and environmental protection with focus on reducing pollution and carbon, further accelerated the construction and digital upgrading of energy storage, transmission and peak shaving system, strengthened the research and demonstration of application of energy-saving and carbon reduction technologies with continued efforts being made to promote advanced and efficient energy-saving products and equipment, and to push forward effectively the improvement of energy utilization efficiency.

1. Energy Infrastructure

（1）Oil and Gas Storage and Transportation Technology

Through the deep integration of new generation sensing, communication and automatic control technologies with various kinds of storage and transportation, oil and gas pipeline transportation, underground and ground storage, natural gas liquefaction and natural gas compression, China has set up a digital technical system of multi-energy storage and transportation with oil and gas storage and transportation technologies as the core technologies. This technical system provides solutions to digitization and intelligence of oil and gas storage and transportation system with comprehensive perception/prediction, adaptive optimization and integrated management and control, meeting the requirements of the information technology for refined oil and gas pipeline transportation, digital storage tank, storage operation and safety monitoring.

Digital Pipeline Network Technology　Through the digital technology of pipeline engineering, pipeline data acquisition and sharing application, through the perception capacity of key pipeline network equipment, real-time data is being obtained, mechanism modeling base built, and the operation trend of pipeline network forecasted; in this way, a digital pipeline network technology system is formed. It assists in improving the operation capacity and reliability of the pipe network; it can also support achieving visual monitoring, network transportation and intelligent management of the pipeline network to ensure the safe and efficient operation of the oil and gas pipeline network. This technology system can meet the needs of digital improvement and intelligent construction of safe transmission and operation management of oil and gas pipeline network from the three aspects of perception, control and decision-making.

Digital Storage Technology　Based on the characteristics that the oil and gas storage system has a fixed plant site, and is associated with different transmission systems (pipeline, railway, shipping and highway), the storage technology system needs to adapt to different storage forms of its media; a digital oil and gas storage management and operation technology system with the ability of operation optimization, risk control and real-time decision-making is constructed through the three-dimensional design and induction system of the oil and gas storage station. This technology provides initial solutions to the informatization challenges in business monitoring, intelligent patrol inspection, metering management and equipment safety in the process of oil and gas storage; it can meet the requirement of oil inventory optimization, safe operation of storage station/warehouse, intelligent maintenance and peak shaving; it can basically realize the continuous optimization of production and operation of various reservoirs, as well as maximization of benefits, efficiency and safety guarantee.

Digital LNG Storage and Transportation Technology Through real-time perception of production data, collection of end consumption data, and in consideration of various factors such as intermittent and volatility features of renewable energy and natural gas market price, a digital control and intelligent decision-making technology system for transportation and marketing of LNG storage and transportation industry is formed. The technology provides initial solutions to the problems in digital operation, safety production, intelligent ship discharge, intelligent gasification and intelligent peak shaving; it supports the maximization of the benefits of LNG production, storage and transportation system.

（2）**Power Grid Technology**

By 2020, China's circuit length of transmission lines of 220 kilovolt and above reached 794,000 kilometer, with the capacity of substation of 220 kilovolt and above being 4.53 billion kVA. A large number of clean energies such as wind power, solar power and hydro power are transmitted from western China to the eastern load center through UHV. China's power grid has been developed into the world largest and most complex grid connected to new energies.[1] Such devices with large capacity multi-circuit technologies are applied on the same power tower, such as carbon fiber composite conductor and other power line technologies; 1000 kilovolt high-voltage AC and ± 1100 kilovolt high-voltage DC technology and complete sets of equipment have reached the international advanced level. Major breakthroughs have been made in key technologies of multi-terminal flexible DC distribution network; microgrid technology has begun to be applied on pilot basis. Great progresses have also been made in power grid information security technology, and

---

[1] Data source: *2021 Annual Development Report of China Power Industry* by China Electricity Council; 2020 data is from the annual statistics of 2020 by China Electricity Council.

technologies such as situation awareness and power grid dispatching have been continuously innovated. Smart grid is applied in modern advanced computer, communication, and networks; sensing and control technologies are applied as well in power system, with features of safety, reliability, green and high efficiency. It improves the safe operation of power grid, power supply reliability, user power supply quality, power grid equipment efficiency and renewable energy utilization efficiency.

Intelligent Power Transmission Technology　This technology mainly includes the dynamic detection and monitoring technology of the transmission system, which has the functions of real-time sensing of the operation status of power tower and transmission line, AI scenario recognition and UAV patrol inspection with the following advantages of improved equipment utilization rate, enhanced transmission safety, increased efficiency in the planning and site/route selection of transmission sites; it also helps reduce casualty rate and labor intensity of operation inspection, significantly improving the power line's resistance against extreme weather disasters such as ice, fire, and typhoon; moreover, it supports quick recovery from any technical breakdowns. The on-line monitoring technology of transmission equipment is applied to achieve accurate positioning of overhead line breakdowns, video monitoring of micro meteorology and mountain fires, while the distributed optical fiber temperature measurement can also be made if necessary. Other tools such as helicopter, UAV are also used to carry out line inspection and realize intelligent operation and maintenance of transmission equipment, with the purpose of eliminating the possibility of safety accidents and quickly locating and handling technical breakdowns.

Intelligent Substation Technology　As per the basic requirements of the digitization of the power station, communication platform and information sharing standardization, the technical system with the functions of automatic information acquisition, measurement, control, protection and monitoring has been developed based on advanced, reliable, integrated and low-carbon intelligent equipment. It can support real-time automatic control of the power grid, intelligent regulation, online analysis and decision-making, and collaborative interaction; the system is able to conduct interaction with adjacent substations and power grid dispatching; it can achieve equipment intelligence, modularization, integration and status visualization; it provides the basic solutions to issues arisen due to un-unified media & protocols and limitations of protocols of conventional substation equipment. With the application of this kind of technology, the following results are accomplished: the primary/secondary integration, real-time detection of operation status of substation, minimization of maintenance problems, and higher operation reliability.

Intelligent Power Distribution Technology　Through the establishment of distribution automation, smart power distribution room and intelligent station area, the technical system has been developed with the functions of distributed feeder automation coverage, optical fiber coverage and primary/secondary integration with the basic characteristics of flexibility, reliability, observability, controllability, openness and compatibility. It provides basic solutions to issues arisen in the smart monitoring, protection, control and management of the distribution system under both normal operation and accident arisen scenarios with improvement in reliability and quality of power supply.

Smart Microgrid Technology Due to the application of computer optimization control system, generator optimization control system and microgrid information acquisition system, the technical system of distributed power generation, energy storage, energy conversion, load and monitoring, safety protection and converter control has been initially established. This technical system has the following characteristics: micro size, flexibility, clean and efficient operation, self-generation/utilization, residual power storage in grid and information optimization. This kind of technology can help solve the problems arisen in self-balancing in power supply, and is able to reduce the impact on the system when connecting the large-scale distributed power supply to the power grid. ensure the stable operation of the smart microgrid system island and fast grid connection. This kind of technology is fit for application of distributed power supply in convenient connection to areas in proximity, industrial parks, remote areas and islands.

（3）Energy Storage Technology

Energy storage technology is mainly used to smooth peak and valley time, to stabilize power fluctuation, and to reduce discarded wind power and solar power. The energy stored can be used for emergency energy, providing basic solutions to the issues of volatility and randomness in the energy system. During the 13th Five-Year Plan period, technologies such as power storage and cooling/heating storage were gradually applied to extensive scales in China; among these technologies, the water pumping and storage technology is the most widely applied.

Cooling/heating Storage Technology Through the storage of cooling exchange energy in devices or media, the technical system is established to realize the functions of storage, release or rapid energy exchange of cooling and heating. This technology has the following characteristics: flexible adjustment in the energy system; high reliability of cooling and heating exchange. It provides solutions to the mismatching problem between supply and demand of cooling and heating in the integrated energy system due to factors such as time, space or intensity; it greatly improves the quality and output of cooling and heating energy, while ensuring safe and stable operation of the integrated energy system. This technology can be applied by users with demand for power and heating peak shaving; it can be used in locations such as energy stations.

Electrochemical Energy Storage Technology   Electrochemical energy storage technology covers different technologies applied in the production of lead-acid battery, lithium-ion battery, sodium sulfur and vanadium flow battery. The installed capacity of lithium-ion battery accounts for 88.8% of China's electrochemical energy storage market, and its application is growing rapidly in the fields of optical storage and integrated charging station, distributed microgrid, frequency modulation auxiliary service, household energy storage. Lithium-ion batteries are mainly made on the basis of technologies such as ternary lithium and lithium iron phosphate, which have the characteristics of high energy density, fast response speed, long cycle life and high conversion efficiency. It can be built in a modular way and is less limited by geographical conditions; it is suitable for mobile equipment, electric vehicles, and renewable energy grid connection.

Water Pumping Storage Technology   The kind of technology refers to that applied in power station that pumps water to an upper reservoir when the reservoir water level is low; when the water level is high, the water is discharged to the lower reservoir for power generation during the peaking time. It has the following characteristics: high water level, large capacity, long service life, mature technology, economy and reliability. Water pumping storage power station can solve the problems of power peak shaving and long-term storage of electric energy in the power system. It helps improve the large-scale renewable energy access capacity, reduce the impact of connecting the renewable energy to the power grid, and achieve efficiency, flexibility, safety and stability in operating a power system.

2. Technology of the Demand Side Energy Saving and Carbon Reduction

（1） The Advancement of Energy-saving Technology in Key Industries Actively Promoted in the Industrial Sectors

China has always attached great importance to technological progress in energy conservation and emission reduction in high energy consuming industries such as iron and steel, nonferrous metals, building materials, petrochemical and pulp. Remarkable results have been achieved. Among these, the comparable energy consumption of large and medium iron and steel enterprises has already reached the advanced level of that in Japan and South Korea; it is also close to the level in Germany; the average power consumption in aluminum production is only 5% higher than the internationally advanced level. However, the energy consumption of some high energy consumption sector is obviously higher; for example, the average energy consumption of cement production is 19% higher than that in Japan, and for papermaking, 90% higher than that in the advanced countries.

The steel, nonferrous metals and other metallurgical sectors have actively adopted various technologies of residual heat and pressure recycling and utilization are applied in the steel, nonferrous metals and other metallurgical industries to recycle residual gas, waste water and other wastes; such applications can not only support energy conservation and emission reduction, but also help reduce production costs and improve product gross profit margin. At the same time, the new generation of information technology is used to improve the traditional production process, to improve the efficiency of metallurgical process, and to achieve energy consumption reduction, emission reduction and quality improvement. The building material sector has been actively promoting green manufacturing, such as advanced grinding technology in cement production that improves energy efficiency in the technical process; moreover, the technologies of steel slag recycling and grinding are applied to replace traditional limestone, which helps with full recycling of wastes; new cement clinker cooling technology and associated equipment are introduced to improve heat recovery efficiency, transportation and operation rate, further reducing power consumption. The petrochemical sector has introduced key technologies commonly used, such as new catalysis, separation and chemical process strengthening; the overall technical level has been significantly improved. This industry has introduced new catalytic materials and technologies, advanced separation materials and technologies, having greatly improved petrochemical production processes; all these have basically streamlined processes, reduced energy consumption and pollution emissions. The pulp sector actively promotes energy-saving and carbon reduction technologies such as residual heat recovery, alkali recovery and medium concentration pulping. Residual heat recovery and utilization technologies include heat recovery from pump drying, preheated mechanical pulp, intermittent cooking and spraying, waste gas from paper machine drying section, flue gas; this has improved overall energy efficiency in the whole production process.

（2）Multi-measures Taken in the Building Industry to Improve Building Structure and Energy Consumption Technology

In the building industry, the end-use application of energy-saving technology is prioritized. For new buildings, green building and investment in green building are promoted:

integrated buildings and passive energy-saving design; energy-saving green materials, prefabricated and steel structure buildings; for existing buildings, the following measures are taken: upgrading of the buildings in terms of energy-saving; improvement of energy efficiency and equipment efficiency. In the upgrading of old residential areas, technical improvements include strengthening the enclosure structure, building thermal insulation and air tightness guarantee for improving the energy-saving potential of the main structures. At the same time, the industry has established an energy efficiency labeling system to provide benchmarking for the purchase of efficient and smart household appliances, refrigerators, lighting and office facilities to reduce energy consumption.

Clean energy cooling and heating technology generally refers to the technical system that uses solar energy, geothermal energy, biomass energy, natural gas and other clean energy to meet the needs of cooling/heating; the kind of technology has been vigorously promoted in the building industry. It has the following characteristics: low-carbon, environmental protection, high efficiency and energy saving. According to the local energy resources/supply conditions, different kinds of cooling/heating can be applied such as heating pump, gas heating and etc. They can be utilized comprehensively so that they are complementary to each other; in this way, the benefits and efficiency are maximized. It can be combined with advanced information and communication technology to solve the problem of coordinated interaction between cooling and heating supply of power grid and heating network, improve the consumption capacity of power grid for renewable energy, and reduce the emission of environmental pollutants. It is suitable for buildings, residents and other scenes with cooling and heating demand. Geothermal energy technology mainly includes three-dimensional seismic survey technology for refined detailed depicting the geological structure of three-dimensional underground space, and the technique of sandstone pore heat storage and recharge, non-raw water re-fill, which guarantees the balanced recovery and irrigation of geothermal water resources; the new generation of information technology, such as automatic data collection and transmission and big data, is also widely used in the development and utilization of geothermal resources in order to further strengthen the monitoring and evaluation of geothermal resources. Biomass energy technology mainly includes high temperature dry and medium to high temperature semi-dry anaerobic fermentation technology, high-efficiency anaerobic fermentation technology, biomass forming fuel machinery manufacturing, special boiler manufacturing, fuel combustion technology. In recent years, with the in-depth promotion of clean heating action, heat pump technologies including air source heat pump, water source heat pump and ground source heat pump have been widely used. Compared with traditional heating methods, heat pumps can integrate biomass heating, steam refrigeration, lighting and heating, and provide efficient/clean cooling and heating supply solutions for regional energy supply.

（3）To Promote Energy Conservation and Efficiency Mainly through Electrification in the Field of Transportation

In the transportation sector, China has a lot of emphasis on the development of EV, high-speed railways and onshore power technologies, with the aim of replacing the traditional fuel devices with electric energy ones, so to achieve significant energy conservation and emission reduction in the transportation industry. The innovations of advanced energy-saving technologies such as braking energy feedback system, ship propulsion system, digital shore power system and transportation system based on advanced information technology are all being actively promoted in an effort of continuously improving energy efficiency.

The fuel economy of traditional fuel vehicles has been continuously improved. By 2020, the average fuel consumption per 100 kilometer of a traditional passenger vehicle has been decreased to 6.67 liters, down more than 30% compared with that of 2015; the fuel consumption of hybrid vehicles has been reduced to 4 liters per 100 kilometer. The technology of electric vehicle is rapidly developed; as a result, the market share, key performance and technical indicators of automobile sector are at the world advanced level. The level of intelligence and networking of smart networked vehicles has been continuously improved, with key software and hardware such as sensors, computing platforms and intelligent cockpits being rapidly updated; independent breakthroughs have been made in basic supporting technologies such as high-precision maps and positioning. China's hydrogen fuel cell technology and related equipment have been developed rapidly. The production technology of proton exchange membrane has basically realized localization; the bipolar plate technology and industrialization capacity have been significantly improved; the metal bipolar plate coating technology has achieved breakthroughs, and a variety of graphite based and titanium chromium based nanocomposite coatings with independent intellectual property rights have been developed; this has laid a solid foundation for the development of hydrogen fuel cell vehicles.

II. New Trends of Energy Technology Revolution Led by Low-carbon Transformation and Digitalization

The increasing demand for combating non-traditional security risks such as climate change, extreme weather, and the Covid-19 epidemic has become an important trend to drive global innovation in scientific and technological development. Innovative breakthroughs in new energy technologies, new materials, and new generation information technologies are not only the main areas of this new round of global technology revolution and industrial transformation, but also inevitable requirements to handle non-traditional security risks. China has proposed the grand goal of becoming one of the top innovative countries by 2035 and a world power in science and technology by 2050. China needs to make full use of its own scientific and technological advantages, industrial advantages, and scale advantages; new opportunities should be searched in the global technological revolution; breakthroughs should be made in all fronts. With focus on the energy technology revolution in China and the guidance of the new national energy security strategy and the "3060" strategic goal, China needs to unswervingly implement the basic national policy of resources conservation and environmental protection, and to unswervingly build a clean, low-carbon, safe and efficient energy system. It is also necessary for China to unswervingly build a new power system with new energy as the core focus. To this end, the future energy technology revolution of China should be towards the direction of taking full advantages of China's digital technology and new energy industry, accelerating the in-depth integration of low-carbon and digital technologies in the energy sector, continuously optimizing energy structures, and improving overall energy efficiency.

i. New Trends in the Development of World Energy Technology

1. New Trends in the Development of Global Green and Low-carbon Technologies to Mitigate Climate Change

As the global consensus on fighting climate change continues to be enhanced, the world's energy supplies will be shifted from traditional fossil energy supplies to a new pattern of diversified development of new energy supplies. The proportion of traditional fossil energy in primary energy will continue to decline-from 85% in 2018 to about 40% in 2050①. The forecasts show that the consumption level of natural gas has not changed much compared with the current level, about 3 to 4 trillion cubic meters per year; but by 2050, oil demand will drop by about 50% compared with 2020; coal consumption will also drop by more than 80%. In contrast, the proportion of clean energy in primary energy consumption will be gradually increased. It is estimated that by 2050, the proportion of renewable energy (including wind, solar, geothermal and biomass) in the primary energy structure will rise from 5% in 2018 to more than 40%, and its consumption will be increased by more than 10 times. Under the general trend of technological progress and investment, as well as reduced costs of new energies but rising carbon prices, it is estimated that by 2050, the demand for nuclear energy will rise by about 100%, and the proportion of hydrogen energy (excluding the non-combustion use of fuel) will reach about 7%.②

In the future, more great progresses shall be made in various energy technologies such as those in exploration, development, storage, transportation, processing, and consumption; the overall technical level of transformation and application will be comprehensively improved. In terms of traditional energy technology, underground in-situ technologies for upgrading, and the technology of re-utilization of abandoned oilfield etc. can greatly improve the efficiency of traditional oil and gas and non-regular oil and gas extraction; the advancement and application of ultra-supercritical thermal power generation technology and advanced IGCC technology can significantly reduce coal consumption for power supply.③ In terms of clean energy technology, wind energy technology innovation is mainly concentrated in high-power energy converters, and wind turbines; the solar technological progresses mainly include those in perovskite solar cells and solar photocatalytic hydrogen production; in hydropower technology, the focus shall be on

---

① Data source: IEA. *World Energy Outlook 2020*. https://www.bp.com/content/dam/bp/country-sites/zh_cn/china/home/reports/bp-energy-outlook/2020/energy-outlook-2020-edition-cn.pdf.pdf.

② Data source: based on the calculation results of the rapid transition scenario in the *World Energy Outlook 2020*.

③ Data source: Sun Xudong, Zhang Bo, Peng Suping. Research on the development trend and strategic countermeasures of China's clean coal technology in 2035. *Engineering Science*, 2020, 22 (3): 132-140.

technologies used in deep-buried large tunnels, prevention technologies against rock bursts, and technologies for tunnel engineering design; in nuclear power technology, the focuses shall be on breakthroughs in nuclear waste treatment and nuclear power station safety technology; positive progresses have already been made in hydrogen energy technologies such as those of photovoltaic hydrogen production, ocean hydrogen transportation, and organic chemical hydrogenation hydrogen storage and transportation system (SPERA); mature geothermal energy exploration technology and high-temperature geothermal energy power generation technology are expected to support the increase in the utilization of geothermal energy.[①] Future digital technologies (such as supercomputing, AI, big data analysis, etc.) can greatly improve the efficiency of energy systems. In particular, the iterative acceleration of technologies with major industrial development prospects in renewable energy is becoming increasingly prominent. Specifically, based on the optimal decision-making model of smart mines, digital technology can effectively support the achievements in safe, efficient, and smart control of all aspects of coal mining activities such as design, production, and operation; combined with existing petroleum exploration technology, the application of intelligent robots can enable a large number of oil and gas resources that could not be exploited due to high cost to be developed technically and economically; the in-depth integration of wind power technology and digital technology will strengthen the smart control of wind turbines and the optimization of power generation; the digitalization of photovoltaic power plants allows asset management, production management, and later operation and maintenance to improve quality and efficiency, in the respects of power plant early warning, anti-risk capabilities, and reducing labor costs; the application of professional standardized data models will improve the development efficiency of geothermal energy and hydropower; digitalization can also greatly facilitate the selection of hydrogen transportation methods, and effectively improve hydrogen's transportation to fit for different transportation scenarios; digital technology is also conducive to on-line monitoring and health management of reactor's pressure vessel performance, and to prolong the life of nuclear power plants.

2. The EU's "Green Policy" Promoting Digital and Green Dual Transformation

For a long time, the EU has been promoting actively its economic and green energy transformation and global climate change governance; its green and low-carbon

---

①   Data source: *World Energy Technology Innovation Direction and Development Trend*.

technology development has always been leading the world in this sector. In the first half of 2019, the EU planed to invest more than 10 billion euros in the "2020-2030 Plan" of the Innovation Fund to support low-carbon technology R&D and innovation; it has the following five aspects: firstly, the renewable energy field, covering floating offshore wind energy technologies such as wind power generation and next-generation wind turbines, solar thermal power generation, organic solar cells, floating photovoltaic devices and other solar energy technologies, enhanced geothermal energy technologies, advanced biofuels and other biological energy technologies, tidal energy and wave energy technologies. Secondly, in the field of energy storage, the innovation includes product innovations such as heat storage, thermal storage and flow batteries, process innovations e.g. block chain and AI, system innovations such as port energy management systems and charging stations, and electrolytic water coupled hydrogen storage systems as well as other large-scale demonstration projects. Thirdly, in the field of Carbon Capture, Utilization and Storage (CCUS), the following aspects are included: full-cycle Carbon Capture and Storage (CCS) projects, partial CCS projects, and other low-carbon technology innovation such as capturing carbon dioxide and other carbon-containing emission gases and converting them into usable fuels or products. Fourthly, for the energy-intensive industrial sectors, such as coke production, oil refining, metals, glass, cement, and chemical production, the innovations are focused on low-carbon technologies. Fifthly, in many cross areas, innovations include low-carbon technology innovation such as multi-factory CCUS, low-carbon hydrogen utilization, hybrid renewable energy systems and heat pump industrial heating systems.

On this basis, in December 2019, the EU issued the "European Green Policy" (referred to as the "Green Policy"), which established a phased goal of reducing greenhouse gas emissions by 50%-55% in 2030 compared with that of 1990 and achieving the long-term goal of weather neutrality by 2050. The "Green Policy" is a comprehensive economic strategy for the EU's medium and long-term sustainable growth. It also further clarifies the EU's seven major development sectors and key tasks for the future development of energy, industry, transportation, construction, and biodiversity. In the energy sector the following are included: the development of renewable energy, the elimination of thermal power, the construction of smart energy facilities; in the industrial sectors, the following are included: accelerated decarbonization of energy-intensive industries; strong support for the development and commercialization of breakthrough technologies such as hydrogen energy; promotion of strategic value chain investment in the battery industry; the development of sustainable digital industries. In the construction industry, the requirements include improving the building renovation rate, exploring for appropriate carbon emission trading system for the building industry, carrying out energy performance contract management in the building industry. In the transportation sector, the requirements include the development of multimodal transportation and the construction of intelligent transportation systems; improvement of the air pollutant emission and carbon dioxide emission standards of ships and airplanes. In the food industry, these include conducting agricultural-ecological performance assessment, reducing the use of pesticides and fertilizers, and strengthening the control of the entire food supply chain. In the ecological sector, the requirements include introduction of stricter biodiversity legislation, the European Union Forest strategy and the development of a sustainable "blue economy", implementation of zero pollution actions in air, water and soil, and sustainable chemical management. Among them, the EU "Green Policy" pays more attention to the intelligent integration of green low-carbon technologies and digital technologies in various fields; it taps the full potential of digital transformation, and accelerates the application of digital technologies such as AI, 5G, cloud computing, edge computing, and the Internet in the respect of energy technology. Although the work arrangements related to the "Green Policy" have been disrupted due to the impact of the Covid-19 epidemic, the EU has always put the strategic investments in the "Green Policy" such as digital infrastructure, clean energy, circular economy, and intelligent transportation systems as the important contents of the "Marshall European Plan" to restore its economy after the epidemic. The EU will also introduce a series of green policies in investment, financing and finance to complement it, such as increasing green investment, expanding green financing, and promoting green finance to ensure the implementation of the "Green Policy".

In the future, the EU member states will work jointly towards the two directions of digitization and greening to further promote the R&D, innovation and application of low-carbon technologies in Europe and the world to achieve its climate goals and tasks.

3. Carbon-neutral Strategy of the United States Accelerating Development of Electric Vehicles and Other New Energy Technologies

Carbon dioxide emissions from energy consumption in the United States, the world's largest economy, peaked as early as 2007 (6.003 billion tons), dropped to 5.146 billion tons in 2019 and further down to 4.574 billion tons in 2020. Since taking office, US president Joe Biden has actively sought for the US leadership in global climate negotiations. He signed an executive order returning the US back to the Paris Agreement immediately after his inauguration, and he announced a new US climate commitment at the Leaders' Summit on Climate on April 22nd, 2021: to reduce greenhouse gas emissions by 50%-52% from 2005 levels by 2030. Meanwhile, the US government proposed "carbon-free power generation by 2035 through a transition to renewable energy; Make America carbon-neutral by 2050".

The US government, for many years, has attached great importance, to research, development and investment in new energy technologies such as EV. the US Department of Energy (DOE) has invested heavily in R&D programs of electric vehicles, including Freedom CAR, Freedom Cooperative Automotive Research, PNGV, Partnership for a New Generation Vehicles, the Advanced Energy Program, and the Advanced Technology Vehicle Manufacturing Loan Program, to undergird R&D of power battery, fuel cell, and lightweight technologies. At the same time, power battery recycling and reuse network was established to minimize energy consumption and waste in electric vehicle sector. In 2019, USDOE set up the first lithium-ion battery (LIB) recycling center, with participation and through concerted efforts of the Oak Ridge National Laboratory, Argonne National Laboratory and other research institutes and enterprises, a closed-cycle of power batteries' recycling and utilization was established in the US. The US will relentlessly promote low-carbon technology in the future, to boost new energy technology development including EV etc. On the one hand, US government plans to invest $2 trillion in clean energy and sustainable infrastructure, $128 million to reduce the cost of solar power generation and develop solar technology, $400 billion to support clean energy R&D and innovation, and a high-level interagency research institute, ARPA-C (ARPA-Climate), is slated to be set up to focus on climate change issues. Financial support for clean energy research and innovation has increased, and the federal investment in CCUS technology was doubled to expedite development and application of CCUS and other technologies. The US government has set in motion the Clean Energy and Sustainability Accelerator to mobilize private-sector to invest in areas such as renewable energy generation. On the other hand, the US has zeroed in on electric vehicles, grid construction and renewable energy etc. Firstly, the US government plans to reorganize factories and ramp up domestic supplies of materials, providing tax incentives to electric car buyers, retrofitting electric school buses and building 500,000 electric charging stations across the country. Secondly, the government sets out to construct a more resilient power grid, raising tax incentives for wind, solar and other renewable energy projects, proactively boosting renewable energy output on public lands and offshore waters, the number of WTGS installed offshore by 2030 is slated to double. Thirdly, to improve energy efficiency and reduce carbon emissions, the US government will focus on renovating and upgrading schools, office buildings, residential buildings and other buildings to promote green buildings and reduce pollution and carbon emissions.

ii. Vision of China's Energy Technology Development

1. Transformation to Low-carbon Energy

Because of differences in energy resources endowment, economic and social development stage between China and developed countries, as well as practical issues such as uneven temporal and spatial distribution of resources and energy demand, China will not, and can not repeat the energy development path of developed countries to realize our future energy revolution. We will surely chart our own path toward developing diversified energy mix as main objective, transforming from a coal-dominated energy mix to a green low-carbon safe and efficient energy system dominated by non-fossil energy. This principle not only crafts inevitable choice for China's energy technology revolution, but also raises imposing challenges. Therefore, we rely on revolution of energy technology to push forward breakthroughs in new energy technology and new technologies in energy sector, fully capitalizing on advantages of digital technology, and realizing deep integration of digitalization and low-carbon development.

Guided by the "3060" strategic objective, China's energy technology revolution will focus on green and low-carbon development with more clarity, its pace will be more steady, and breakthroughs will be expedited in basic energy theories, technological chains and industrial structures. Carbon peaking will be realized before 2030 in China, breakthroughs in new technologies will be promoted continuously in traditional energy sector, such as ultra-high water head and ultra-low water head turbine design, R&D of high-temperature advanced materials for gas turbines, heavy gas turbines and single-cycle small gas turbines, CCUS technology with high efficiency and low cost for thermal power, small modular reactors, fast reactors, molten salt reactors and other new generation of advanced nuclear power technologies. Technologies in new energy sector will develop by leaps and bounds, such as industrialization of crystal silicon technology of high efficiency and low cost, high parameter solar thermal power generation technology, key technology and equipment for large-scale WTGS, offshore wind power system design and construction technology, low-cost and low wind velocity wind power generation technology, fuel cell distributed generation technology, tidal power generation technology, hot dry rock power generation technology, etc., and high-precision, long-scale new energy power prediction technology, high proportion of distributed new energy status sensing and control technology, all afore-mentioned technologies will make new energy rapidly growing from a supplementary role to one of those main energy sources, supplying most of the incremental energy demand. Carbon neutrality will be achieved by 2060, deepening of China's energy technology revolution will give rise to creation of a new system with green energy knowledge and technology. Commensurate with this goal, an energy technology architecture rested on "Internet plus" smart energy will be basically completed by then, constituting a power supply technology system mainly based on "renewable energy plus flexible resources", coupled with non-electricity supply technology system dominated by clean and efficient utilization of fossil energy, CCUS and hydrogen energy. To this end, we need to push forward rapid iteration of energy storage technology, and to strongly shore up speedy expansion of renewable energy and electric vehicles. Breakthroughs should be accelerated in key technologies and equipment along industrial chain of hydrogen energy. We should give full play to our advantages of nation-wide mobilization mechanism, to localize and industrialize CCUS technology, so as to efficiently recycle and reuse carbon emissions in the fields of industry, construction and transportation, thus in the end attain the goal of carbon neutrality with contribution of carbon sinks.

2. Development of Key Technologies

(1) Technologies in Fields of Renewable Energy and New Energy

It is expected that by 2030, China's primary energy demand will peak and reach a plateau, with an energy mix optimized at an accelerated pace. Non-fossil energy will surpass coal to become the largest primary energy source after 2035, contributing to more than 2/3 of the total primary energy demand by 2050. Continuous expansion of new energy industries such as solar energy, wind power, biomass, geothermal energy, tidal power, the third and fourth generation of nuclear energy will promote innovative development of new energy technologies and equipment, in a sustainable manner.

Specifically, research on solar technology focuses on perovskite solar cells, multi-stack solar cells, solar photocatalytic hydrogen production, catalysts, semiconductor electrodes, etc. The research hotspots of wind energy technology include high power energy converter, wind turbine, wind power numerical simulation, stable grid connection of high proportion of wind power, etc. The research of biomass technology targets at lignin pyrolysis, catalyst, pretreatment, microalgae biofuel, bio-refining, cellulose biofuel and so on. Energy storage research prioritizes on lithium ion battery, sodium ion battery, lithium sulfur battery, anode and cathode materials, quick-charging technology and other options. Geothermal technology research is concentrated on enhanced geothermal system, geothermal system numerical simulation, geothermal drilling technology and so on. Nuclear energy technology studies are centered on nuclear waste treatment technology, nuclear power plant safety technology, irradiation-resistant materials, small nuclear reactor technology etc.

（2）New Power System

The new power system is the one where new energy plays a key role in production and consumption, with coordinated development of various power grids. It is green and low-carbon, diversified and interactive, flexible and agile, synergetic and efficient, digitalized and intelligent, safe and controllable. Driven by energy revolution in China, distributed new energy sources and electric vehicles have been on a development path by leaps and bounds, accelerating changes of power distribution and power consumption pattern. A large number of electric and electronic equipment are connected to grid, resulting in drastically reduced inertia of the system and daunting challenges to safe and stable operation of the system. To tackle this problem, research on new type of power system will be focused on two aspects of technological breakthroughs.

Firstly, integration of diverse energy sources and multi-network convergence. The new power system is shored up by a diversified energy mix tailored to different local conditions, where new technologies such as hydrogen and energy storage will be applied on a large scale, electric energy, thermal energy and cold energy serving as synergetic complement to each other. Equal importance is attached to system of "large base + large power grid" and that of "distributed power+microgrid" simultaneously, to achieve a high degree of integration of a variety of energy infrastructure networks. On supply side, a high proportion of new energy shall be widely connected, and cross-domain resourcesneed be allocated in a flexible and reliable way to ensure smooth connection of various distributed energy facilities. On demand side, peak-valley difference and volatility are augmented, users are not only energy producers and consumers, but also participants in the power balance, which entails in-depth synergetic interaction of generation-grid-load-storage of power, shifting from "load-oriented generation" to "generation-led load" to "interaction between generation and load", making "integration of diverse energy sources and holistic synergy of power output" possible.

We need to break the bottleneck of stability control of power system connected with high proportion of new energy and powered electronic equipment, as well as the basic theory of risk decision-making. An intelligent distribution system, adaptive to characteristics of new energy, with greatly improved ability of new energy power forecast shall be constructed in an all-round way. Through digitalized, web-based and intelligent system, high-degree integration of various energy sources will be promoted, leading to huge improvement of flexibility and controllability of powered electronic equipment, to effectively address uncertainty of power system, and improve system's ability to defend itself. Potential in demand side response should be further released, generation-grid-load-storage system shall be optimized in an overall sense, to achieve extensive interconnection and intelligent interaction of power system.

（3）Technologies in the Field of Hydrogen Energy

Hydrogen energy is a kind of secondary energy with wide sources, clean and flexible in use, with a myriad of application scenarios. Hydrogen technology covers a series of comprehensive technological disciplines such as basic material science, equipment manufacturing and infrastructure construction. At present, hydrogen industry is in the early stage of development, so we need to pay close attention to three areas.

There are three technical routes for hydrogen production. The "grey hydrogen" route of traditional fossil energy production will be restricted, while hydrogen produced as industrial by-product via hydro-met coking process, chlor-alkali and propane dehydrogenation will be put in the spotlight. The "blue hydrogen" process combining fossil energy and CCUS technology is expected to become an important option. The "green hydrogen" route, where hydrogen is produced from renewable energy, is the future of hydrogen development, it includes alkaline water electrolysis, proton exchange membrane electrolysis and solid oxide electrolysis technologies. Non-electrolytic hydrogen production routes such as solar thermal and nuclear hydrogen production are being explored.

Many problems concerning hydrogen storage and transportation need to be solved. Hydrogen storage and transportation technology with high efficiency and low consumption is the priority of future scientific research. On the one hand, the high-pressure gaseous hydrogen storage technology is basically full-fledged, high-pressure autoclave materials with better performance are being developed to improve pressure grade and reduce the tank weight. In the field of R&D on low temperature liquid hydrogen storage, the focus is on efficient thermal insulation containers and liquefied low energy consumption technology and equipment; breakthroughs need to be made to reduce cost and lower power consumption of dehydrogenation catalysts in terms of organic liquid hydrogen storage. Solid material hydrogen storage technology relies on breakthrough in area of hydrogen storage medium with low melting point, to greatly improve the quality and efficiency of hydrogen storage index. On the flip side, pipeline hydrogen transport is still facing barriers such as material hydrogen embrittlement, and pipeline transport experiments of mixing natural gas with hydrogen are being carried out, as a result, large-scale indirect hydrogen transport may be realized in the future.

We still need to make breakthroughs in technology of terminal use of hydrogen. On the one hand, fuel cell is expected to become an important power supply for future transportation and building energy use. Fuel cell does not only provide clean energy for high-power transportation equipment, but also participates in cogeneration and peak regulation of power, which is conducive to coordinated and optimized operation of system with multiple energy sources. In addition, hydrogen-fueled internal combustion engine technology, especially aviation fuel technology, will also be researched and applied. On the other hand, demand of hydrogen in field of smelting and chemical industries is expected to grow significantly. Hydrogen and other relevant technologies are being tested and promoted as a reducing agent to replace coke in iron-making process, and as a chemical raw material to absorb CO_2.

（4）Technologies in the Field of CCUS

CCUS refers to a technology that uses certain methods to capture and transport man-induced emissions of carbon dioxide to specific locations for utilization or storage. It is estimated that China is to emit about 1.5 billion tons of carbon dioxide by 2060, so CCUS technology is needed to realize carbon neutrality by then.

The most advanced and widely used CCUS technologies are chemical absorption (such as ethanolamine compounds) and physical separation (the adsorbent is released by temperature or pressure changes). Among which, technology of separating or capturing carbon dioxide from flu gas has been commercialized; good result is yielded in carbon dioxide capturing of industrial tail gas in sectors of cement, coal chemical industry, petrochemical industry, coking, IGCC etc. Thanks to advancement of polymer or inorganic device (membrane) technology with high carbon dioxide selectivity, the carbon dioxide capture technology of flue gas with low concentration in power plants is expected to be applied on a large scale.

Carbon dioxide geological sequestration technology includes saline aquifer sequestration, coal seam sequestration, marine sequestration and so on. Safe and environmental-friendly intelligent storage is realized through intelligent selection of site, intelligent injection-production and real-time monitoring all the way from drilling to injection, from static evaluation to dynamic simulation. Specifically speaking, fine simulation and evaluation are conducted via static modeling, geomechanical modeling, and dynamic mathematical modeling before compressed carbon dioxide is injected into rock structures with specific geological conditions (depleted oil and gas fields, deep coal seams, deep underground aquifers and other geological environments). Siting, injection and operation simulation are carried out based on characteristics of carbon dioxide storage. Cap rock integrity is analyzed and evaluation is done on fault activation risk, and wellbore integrity, etc.

Carbon dioxide utilization technology mainly includes oil and gas recovery technology and chemical engineering technology. Firstly, through intelligent gas injection equipment and oil and gas fracturing equipment, oil and gas stimulation technology can improve reservoir pressure and oil flow, to realize carbon dioxide fracturing, carbon dioxide flooding and partial storage. Secondly, carbon dioxide can be used to make plastics degrade. Blending with green hydrogen, carbon dioxide can produce fertilizer and other petrochemical products; such technologies are expected to be widely used. Things are looking up for microalgae carbon sequestration to produce bio-oil and feed.

iii. Trend of Development of Key Digital and Low-carbon Integrated Technologies

Our objective is to build a clean, low-carbon, intelligent and efficient, economically secure energy system, through step-by-step convergence of traditional energy technologies and digital technologies, accelerating breakthroughs in smart unmanned mines, smart oil fields, smart factories, smart storage and transportation and other technical fields, promoting transition of traditional fossil energy to green and low-carbon energy. A new power system underpinned by new energy is to be constructed through deep fusion of digital and intelligent technology with new energy technology; improvements shall be sustained in smart power generation, smart grid, smart power storage, smart consumption and other technical areas, thus increasing renewable energy share, gradually enhancing energy efficiency, further lifting level of safe operation of energy systems and realizing integration of multiple energy sources, eventually, creating a smart energy systems connecting complete cycle of production, supply, storage and consumption in collaborative manner.

1. Digital Technology

Data, in new development stage, working as a new factor of production, is combined with capital, human resources, energy resources and other factors to promote digital development of energy industry. We should leverage integration and innovation of new generation information technology, including digital technology, communication technology and AI, with energy technology, striving to solve problems of extensive growth, low efficiency, high pollution and high carbon emissions in the energy sector. We should start with research and consulting, architecture design, data governance and technical solutions, through application of advanced technologies such asintellisense, edge computing, intelligent connection, smart platform and application, with hopes of establishing a new business model integrating multiple energy sources and data. These technologies are applicable to a full range of business scenarios from energy production, processing, transmission, storage and consumption, to carbon management and trading.

（1）Intellisense and Cloud Edge Synergy

Intelligent sensing employs advanced sensing technology to convert field environmental information of energy into digital value, which, will be processed and calculated by intelligent terminal and then transmitted to platform via network. Intelligent sensing works with cloud edge to handle information collection, transmission and processing in various energy environments.

Sensor Technology　　Energy sensors, capable of capturing complex and diverse characteristics of a mechanism, can convert feature parameters, environment and human features along links of production, transmission, storage and consumption into electrical signals and digital quantities. Energy sensors are operated in complex environment, subject to various strong interference signals, hence high requirement on low power consumption and long life cycle. It is imperative for us to solve the following technical problems of different sensors, including material, microstructure, manufacturing process performance, digital processing, surface modification, reliability, weather resistance, low power consumption and so on. Various new sensing materials, sensing mechanism and high-precision sensing components and parts are to be studied. Energy sensors are applied to exploration, exploitation, transportation and consumption of fossil energy, as well as scenarios like power generation, transmission, transformation, distribution and consumption. When condition of sites does not allow sensors to be installed, video image analysis can be applied to obtain perceptual information.

Micro Source Energy Harvesting　　According to local conditions, solar energy, wind power, heat, mechanical vibration, electrical energy and other micro energy can be converted to power sensor networks. It is highly intensified technology, integrating various technologies. We need to do problem-shooting on following issues: performance of captive power supply for sensors, battery performance and safety, therefore, a series of technology research needs to be carried out in fields of electromagnetic compatibility design, lamination integration, structural design and life cycle extension measures. Micro source energy, integrated with sensors and sensor networks, can be installed in places with lighting, wind, vibration, heat, electric energy and so on.

Low Power-consuming Wireless Sensor Network   Wireless sensor networks can provide two typical communication modes: long-distance wide-area coverage, star networking and medium-short-distance local coverage; self-organizing multi-hop network forwarding. The former one has low transmission rate, but boasts low deployment cost, high terminal access, and both long distance coverage and low working power, while the latter delivers high transmission rate, yet short transmission distance, low access capacity, low power, and strong anti-interference performance, therefore, lightweight gateways and protocols are required. Sensor networks need to ensure low (ultra low) power consumption, stable online rate, and lessor free maintenance of network. Studies should be focused on energy saving design of sensor and network hardware, and software design method, operating strategy to realize ultra-low energy consumption of nodes and network transmission, as well as the wireless transmission power control technology. Low-power wide area network is suitable for field data transmission scenarios of various energy sources, and is widely used in scenarios of mines, oil and gas fields, and power plant, power grids, especially those with harsh environment and high labor costs.

Edge Intelligent Terminal   In some scenarios, communication technology is inadequate in terms of delay and bandwidth, resulting in mismatch of computing capability of cloud platform side and computing demand of the terminal side. Therefore, edge computing is needed to sink the computing capability to terminal node, making terminal side intelligent. Problems remained to be solved include edge computing, storage, security and cloud-side collaboration. Studies should be conducted on the following technologies: state characterization, information model, identification and positioning, and multidimensional perception data fusion analysis of energy sensor networks, which are suitable for complex computing scenarios with delay and bandwidth sensitivity.

(2) Intelligent Connection

Data transmission network between smart terminal and smart platform will deliver a better data transmission service at a higher rate and higher Service Level Agreement (SLA), 5G, F5G, IPv6 + intelligent network management, as well as other communication technology combination, can meet energy data transmission demand of all scenarios, seamless coverage is possible with respect to low latency, reliability, and security, etc. In the future, we need to work out solutions for all kinds of network access and intelligent network management, as well as transmission, security and timeliness of massive energy data.

Intelligent Communication Network Management Communication network is monitored through integration of communication network management control technology, platform technology, terminal technology and AI technology; so network resources can be configured automatically, achieving data path adjustment, quick forecast and analysis of network bugs and problem-shooting, and evaluation of network security and performance, realizing network planning, construction, operation, maintenance in an intelligent way, across-the-board cross-regional network stratified management, and massive terminal access and SLA guarantee. Regarding this technology, we need to solve problems such as access, management, security, and operation and maintenance (O&M) of massive energy network elements and terminals. It is suitable for data transmission and communication network in scenarios requiring high SLA guarantee and reliability.

5G Communication Technology This technology is featured with high directional transmission, high gain, and strong anti-interference performance; it can eliminate multiple interference, realize flexible configuration of parameters such as carrier interval, improve system capacity, provide end-to-end service security isolation, and differentiated end-to-end service experience for users and businesses. The peak rate of this technology can reach more than 20 gigabit/per second, with communication time delay being less than 1 millisecond, and being able to support 1 million devices access per square kilometer. It can provide high speed, large bandwidth, low latency, large capacity, high mobility, wide area coverage, high density, meeting requirements of various industrial applications in terms of spectrum and other technical performance index. Problems need to be solved: wireless transmission, security, time-effectiveness and other problems of massive energy data. This technology can be widely used in smart mines, smart oil fields, smart power grids, smart factories, zero-carbon parks and other scenarios.

F5G Technology This technology is based on Optical Transport Network (OTN), Gigabit Passive Optical Network (GPON), 10 Gigabit Passive Optical Network (XGPON), and other optical transmission technology. A new generation of all-optical fixed network communication technology is formed, comprising Optical Time Domain Reflecto Meter (OTDR), Fiber Doctor/Optical Doctor (FD/OD) and other fiber maintenance technologies, optical fiber sensing (vibration, temperature, offset)/fiber optic monitoring technologies, demonstrating stronger business delivery capacity, higher stability, safety and reliability.

Technical barriers include: big industrial Internet bandwidth (2 megabit- 100 gigabit per second), low latency (50 milliseconds), the high reliability (ring protection), passive remote access, explosion-proof, etc. It will be applied in infrastructure of foundation-bearing network for future optical communication, while it can also be applied to long-distance passive industrial optical ring network communication in coal mines, optical fiber safety early warning for oil and gas pipelines, grid information communication backbone network and other scenarios.

"IPv6 +" Communication Technology　"IPv6 +" is a collection of a series of innovative agreements, catering to the needs of 5G/IoT era on Internet Protocol (IP) data bearing network, including SRv6 based on IPv6 forwarding plane, network fragmentation, end-to-end transmission quality, intelligent traffic tuning technology and other typical technologies, making it the bearer network of next generation, which is intelligent, simplified, automatic and SLA-committing. This technology shores up the weakness of IP protocol, whereas we need to solve problems such as network transmission delay, jitter, packet loss, to ensure reliability in transmission process. It will be widely used in production network and office network of various energy enterprises.

（3）Smart Platform

This technology is underpinned by energy data and smart applications, providing computing, storage, cloud platform and energy public cloud services and other IT infrastructure and components serving as necessary means for production and operation, helping improve quality and efficiency of energy industry and create value for the sector, supporting innovation and development of the industrial chain and ecosystem. Technical barriers include: platform architecture, IT public service, energy public cloud service and so on.

Computing Techniques　The development of computing technology will continuously improve processing speed of CPU, numerical computing ability and integration. By making the server more intelligent, we can shatter CPU's constraint on server computing power, delivering efficient computing power for different Workload. Classic computing technologies will continue to evolve at current speed and scale, and will encounter bottlenecks; thus it is necessary to explore and research on ground-breaking computing technologies such as quantum computing.

Data Storage Technology　As an important component of smart energy infrastructure, by improving storage density per unit of space and energy consumption, this technology improves data read/write performance and processing efficiency, as well as provides a more secure data storage solution to ensure space, use and security of data. It boasts large bandwidth, low latency, high storage density, high reliability, large capacity and other technical features. Its data access bandwidth reaches petabytes level, access time delay at μs level, data storage at level ZB, data reliability at 99.9999%, neither loss of data nor business interruption in fault scenarios, being able to meet storage requirements of various kinds of industry application. Technical barriers are: storage cost, reading efficiency, data reliability and security of massive data.

Cloud Platform　Based on IT hardware and software resources, the Cloud platform provides computing, network, and storage capabilities with advantages such as low cost, large scale, flexible scale-up, and high reliability; it is the base of digital infrastructure of the energy industry. The platform is more responsive, and thus its computing power, algorithm, application and other enabling capabilities are increasingly shared and service-oriented, with both security and impact resistance being taken into account. The platform offers a variety of architectures, including modeling tools, data quality management tools, and fault analysis tools that can quickly turn applications into services. For this technology to work, we need to address technical issues of seamless synchronization of public and private cloud and many other kinds of cloud, data exchange across the board, data security and privacy protection on an open sharing platform, security monitoring and attack-defense, develop data model, data and quality management tools, further enhancing collaborative dispatching of system resources, public service and development, etc.

Energy Public Cloud Service　Platform as a Service (PaaS), Software as a Service (SaaS), data processing, and industry model are key elements of energy public cloud services, which can bolster fast access of big data, AI and block chain to smart applications. Large-scale access of energy data and the all-domain sharing of business data and applications are basic building blocks of public cloud services, which entails fluidity of energy data along links of construction, management, operation and maintenance, eliminating data silos, demarcating data security boundaries and unifying data models. Technical barriers: how to realize rapid construction and response of public cloud services, large-scale access of energy data and sharing of data and application, fast delivery of data integration and application and supporting tools. Research needs to be done on energy data model, digital twin information model, real scenario and entity modeling, reconstruction and other data models.

（4）Smart Applications

On top of platform and data, this technology employs AI, big data, block chain and other technologies to control and manage operations through robots, UAVs and intelligent analysis, to create value. Machine cognitive learning, logical reasoning and intelligent decision-making are technical problems still pending for solution.

Big Data Applications Based on advanced information technology, it can extract, handle, process, analyze correlation of multi-dimensional, huge amount of data, revealing inherent law of interaction between energy and economy, environment and people's livelihood, offering timely feedback and analysis results, to help deal with needed information for energy production, operation and market exchange, and benefit government regulation and enterprise management decision. Technical barriers are: data island, inconsistent standards, difficulty in processing massive big data and poor applicability of models. It is suitable for a series of cross-sectoral data analysis scenarios such as industry climate index, urban load hot spots, user credit and value analysis, and industry development trend.

Artificial Intelligence Applications Combined with robot, UAV, intelligent recognition of image, auxiliary decision-making support and other technologies, AI technology can change traditional energy production and operation mode, so that part of energy production control and operation system is able to do independent analysis, control, decision-making and other intelligent behaviors. Technical issues are: operation, analysis, control and decision-making which are conducted by machines instead of men; as a result, we need to further study energy domain knowledge map and cognitive reasoning, intelligent recognition, intelligent decision-making on control and consolidation of collective intelligence and human-machine optimized decision-making, etc. This kind of technology can be used in grid, UAS inspection of long-distance pipeline and robot operation in underground mine, and other highly risky manual tasks such as working at heights on power grid, underwater drilling robot, and rescue robot.

Block Chain Applications Energy block chain is a distributed accounting method applied to energy industry. Transactions and records are logged in a secure and transparent way. Activities of any node are supervised by other nodes, making fraud impossible. Data can be exchanged anonymously without the need for each other's identities and personal information. Problems need to be solved: authenticity and security of energy data and no-tampering of data in energy trading. It is applicable for distributed energy trading, energy asset trading, carbon management and transaction, etc.

2. Smart Energy Technologies

Green low-carbon transformation of energy development in the future entails accelerated energy technology revolution. Deep integration of new technology in energy sector, new energy sources and advanced ICT should be promoted, gradually putting into place an intelligent technical system connecting energy production, processing, transmission, storage and use. A more intelligent and fully-developed system covering production, supply and consumption of fossil energy will be set up consequently, alongside a more intelligent and synchronized continuum of generation-grid-load-storage for non-fossil energy. Proportion of new energy in energy mix will gradually increase to more than 50%, with improved utilization efficiency, better energy conservation and emission reduction effect, which provides strong technical support for energy production and consumption revolution.

（1）Smart Power Generation

Deep integration of power generation technology and new generation of digital technology gave rise to smart power generation technology system, which enjoys higher automatically controlled output, remote monitoring, convenient maintenance and other features. This kind of technology can improve flexibility of matching load demand and output to a certain extent, thus being more suitable for the construction of new power system with new energy as the centerpiece. However, its growth is hindered by high volatility, susceptibility to weather, low inertia and so on, which can easily cause random output, thus making it difficult to align with peak demand load. Therefore, it is necessary to raise efficiency of renewable energy, shave volatility of new energy output, and improve reliability and stability of power output on supply side.

Smart Photovoltaic Power Station Technology Intelligent PV power station is comprised of intelligent photovoltaic modules, cluster inverter, photovoltaic controller, operation and maintenance cloud center, etc. It is characterized with ability of new energy power generation forecast, intelligent monitoring system, intelligent current and voltage (IV) diagnosis, AI machine learning, intelligent cleaning by robot, UAV inspection and so on. We need to improve conversion efficiency, level of unmanned operation and deep integration with meteorological big data in multi-application scenarios and complex terrain environment. Moreover, issues in solar power station output, curtailment and absorption of those output also need to be solved. This kind of technology is applicable in mountainous areas, floating power stations and water surfaces where manual detection on components are difficult and costly, lowering the bar of siting photovoltaic power stations.

Smart Wind Farm Technology It has the following functions and features: intelligent design, field cluster centralized monitoring, intelligent fault diagnosis, forecast and early warning via big data, preventive maintenance, Augmented Reality (AR) inspection, end-to-end field cluster performance management, etc.; disturbance immunity, adaptability and economic viability. For this technology to work, we need to solve problems of remote operation and maintenance of, low speed, high altitude and offshore wind power system in complex terrains to identify loss factors of wind power; we need to increase utilization rate of power generation, improve the wind farm operation efficiency, and reduce cost of power generation. The technology can be applied in complex terrains such as hills and hilltops, special environments with low wind speed, high altitude and low temperature, as well as site selection, assembly, installation, maintenance and operation of onshore and offshore wind farms.

Smart Nuclear Power Technology   Intelligent diagnosis and analysis algorithm are used on key equipment to come up with operation and maintenance strategy. It is characterized by integrated, intelligent, and secure operation with less manual work. Technical issues include: inability to make right and timely judgment for nuclear power plant fault in complex working conditions, resulting in serious accidents due to failure of taking right measures; ability to provide automat forecast, detection, diagnosis, prediction, to put forward suggestions in a complex environment, with a view to improve safety and availability of plant. It can be applied in extreme scenarios such as tsunami resistance, external flood, large aircraft crash.

（2）Smart Grid

By virtue of deep integration of physical power grid and digital grid, smart grid boaststhe following features: two-way fluidity between power and information, highly automatic, highly flexible, real-time information exchange, etc. It can effectively solve the problem of stability mechanism changes brought by high degree of electronization of electric power, ensure stable operation of the system under condition of high proportion of new energy grid connection and high degree of electrification of terminals and distributed load, as well as to smooth out fluctuations of power market price. It can further improve safety, reliability/flexibility of power supply, and enhance power quality and energy efficiency.

Smart Power Transmission Technology   Through integrated application of small and micro smart sensors and IoT sensing terminals, AI platform, power electronics technology, this technology can put key transmission facilities located in remote areas under control and regulation via digital real-time sensing, creating dynamic digital twins, thus changing forms of information of transmission network, making it intelligent, data driven, anti-interference, panoramic view, holographic decision-making, whole process control, etc. Technical barriers: how to realize rapid positioning, fault diagnosis, recovery, all-weather unmanned inspection, flexible manpower repair in digital form, increase AI inspection recognition rate, overcome difficulty in power supply, make it more interference resistant and less susceptible to environment. It is suitable for transmission network with wide cross-domain, in complicated topography and climate conditions, with robust transmission capability.

Intelligent Transformer Technology It has become the hub of a variety of energy interaction, realizing multi-dimensional perception, analysis and decision-making on interwoven energy network and power grid, performing unmanned intelligent operation. It is featured withthe following functions: integrated unification of digital platform and multi-system multi-terminal, integration of primary and secondary equipment, software defined terminal, remote online upgrade, real-time perception of equipment status, etc. Through integration of digital technology and flexible DC technology, it can handle voltage instability, broadband oscillation, decreased inertia, and frequency instability induced by large-scale new energy access. We need to overcome technical barriers in holographic real-time information capturing with ease, effective analysis of huge amount of data and intelligent decision-making on operation and maintenance. It can be applied to scenarios with large-scale new energy grid-connection, flexible comprehensive energy connectivity in large cities, ocean island and platform power supply, etc.

Smart Power Distribution Technology By means of edge computing terminal, local data storage, computing and analysis and other technical means, it achieves low power consumption, wide coverage, low cost, free of life cycle maintenance and other goals. It presents large proportion of electronized power, complex and diverse network structure, multi-source power supply network, two-way energy flow and energy mutual aid of feeder group. We need to solve problems of regulation and control of distributed energy, whole life cycle equipment monitoring, fault self-diagnosis and restoration, islanding, power quality management, demand response. We need to improve on-line state detection and intelligent level of inspection of O&M of distribution network equipment, creating a safe and reliable, green and smart, efficient distribution network, building a future-focused, interactive, new type of distribution network system integrating generation, grid, load and storage.

Intelligent Scheduling Operation Technology Because large-scale renewable energy output is not controllable with high volatility, intelligent dispatching management technology shifts its target from power supply to load demand, from transmission side to distribution side of power system, unlocking a large number of distributed flexible resource to use, through situational awareness and digital twin technology, to synchronize generation, grid and load. It has the characteristics of compliance, refinement, and information transparency. However we still need to solve problems of real-time scheduling, collaborative interaction of generation-grid-load-storage, power balance, smooth fluctuation, reduced faults and so on.

Virtual Power Plant Technology   By means of measurement technology, regulation technology and communication technology, it can consolidate, coordinate and optimize geographically dispersed distributed resources, participate in power market and auxiliary service market, manage and provide auxiliary services for distribution and transmission network. Technical barriers include: difficulty in scheduling distributed resource and insufficient installed capacity in some areas. Function wise, virtual power plants can be divided into commercial ones and technical ones. Regarding commercial virtual power plants, we do not factor its impact on distribution network into consideration, and it can join power market in the similar way as traditional power plants. From the perspective of system management, technology-based virtual power plant weighs up real-time impact of aggregated resources on local network.

（3）Smart Power Storage

Through a series of technologies such as storage virtualization and fine control, it can operate in conjunction with new energy stations, substations and new loads. It features fast charging and discharging, flexible and intelligent, standardized, module-based andsoftware-definable. Technical issues include: impact of random, intermittent and unstable new energy on power system and energy storage system security, compatibility and other issues. We need to improve utilization rate of power generation equipment, assist peak-shaving, enhance control level of distribution network, improve grid stability, to support grid connection and absorption of new energy.

Intelligent Light Storage Technology   AI, cloud computing technology and photovoltaic, are deeply fused with intelligent group string energy storage technology, which is based on distributed storage system architecture, energy optimization on battery module level, energy control of single battery cluster, digital intelligent management, and whole-module design technology. It can realize fine management and control of battery module featuring optimization as per each pack, management as per each cluster, reducing cost of leveling energy storage while initiating more discharge at the same time. The technology, string-formed, intelligent, module-based, presents high economic performance, safe, reliable, and intelligent operations with long service life. We need to work out a solution regarding large-scale renewable energy grid connection, raising power quality, grid load regulation, and safe operation. It can be applied to ground-based power plant, household green electricity, industrial green power, off-grid island network and other scenarios.

Smart Pumped Storage Power Station   Intelligent management is implemented based on whole lifecycle data collected in respect to survey and design of pumped storage power station design, civil construction, mechanical and electrical installation and O&M, to achieve information digitization, network-based communication, consolidated standardization, conformant operation, business interaction, optimal operation, intelligent decision-making, to enhance intelligent level of construction and O&M of the unit, and to promote paradigm shift from planned maintenance to flexible maintenance. It ensures fast response, swift power regulation, flexible operation and high safety level. Latent defects and safety risks in power station construction and operation should be eliminated so as to boost absorption of clean energy.

Cloud Energy Storage Technology Various technologies such as data analysis, optimization and prediction are applied to assemble energy storage devices scattered on user side onto cloud for conformant scheduling and maintenance. Grid scheduling or physical energy storage on user side is displaced by virtual energy storage capacity on the cloud. On the basis of power grid, cloud energy storage deeply integrates sharing economy with power system,being virtual, sharing, consistent and transmissible. Technical barriers include: how to share energy storage resources to the maximum extent, make sure power grid or users do not need to deliberately purchase energy storage devices, due to better use of existing idle energy storage, gather a large number of complementary users and achieve economies of scale.

（4）Smart Electricity Use

Accurate and timely collection of relevant information, analysis of power consumption data, plus understanding of users' power consumption behavior and status can improvestatistical efficiency and quality of power data, raise power consumption efficiency, effect of energy conservation and emission reduction. This technology is highlighted in intelligent metering, intelligent data-collection, high-speed communication, terminal interaction, etc. We still need to solve problems concerning latent electrical safety risks, peak-load shaving, low system efficiency, and to achieve multiple load interaction, high electrification, rapid demand response, and so on. Demand side response is a mechanism changing user's energy use pattern, adjusting their energy consumption behavior through market price signaling or incentives, to effectively curb the grid volatility.

Integrated Construction Technology of Photovoltaic Power Generation and Storage, Charging, DC and Flexible Load This technology is comprehensive, efficient, flexible, turning power load from rigid to flexible, driving mode from AC to DC, building sector from power user to producer/consumer. We need to address the problem of energy loss caused by continuous AC and DC conversion of photovoltaic power generation, buildings' power systems, and repeated connection to conversion devices. The "PV+ DC+ intelligent charging pile" technology can reduce capacity of medium and low voltage power grid transmission and distribution, while DC powered buildings with energy storage can improve energy use efficiency.

Electric Vehicle V2G (Vehicle-to-Grid) Technology V2G is a two-way interaction technology between electric vehicles and power grid, including electric vehicle charging technology, battery discharge technology to grid, connectivity technology synchronizing smart grid and electric vehicle, etc. As temporary mobile and distributed energy storage facilities, electric vehicles can realize peak-shaving and valley-filling through orderly charging and discharging, feeding power to the grid at peak time and charging from it at low time, which can effectively improve the operation efficiency and resource allocation capability of the grid.

Green Smart Data Center Power Use Technology Based on DC power distribution, UPS on-demand configuration, intelligent battery management, etc., the technology can reduce energy consumption of data center, streamline management, and reduce costs. Working with renewable energy power supply solutions and demand side management, it can increase renewable energy use and mitigate grid fluctuations. Thanks to modular data center solution and resource consolidation, it can drastically cut back on physical space occupancy rate and effectively reduce overall energy consumption and power usage effectiveness (PUE). Intelligent O&M platform shifts paradigm from panoramic monitoring to automatic monitoring, from rule-based malfunction detection to failure prediction based on AI machine learning.

(5) Smart Oil and Gas Exploration and Development

The technologies of intelligent sensor, intelligent analogy, knowledge map, machine learning are being applied in oil and gas exploration and development, putting up together an integrated operation model of reservoir geology, engineering and production. Deep learning and training are conducted on top of massive sample data, to achieve rapid and intelligent identification and evaluation on reservoir's physical property information, real-time tracking and intelligent monitoring on engineering design and construction of drilling and completion, intelligent diagnosis and early warning of shaft engineering accident, etc. Problems need to solve: data silos, software fragmentation and AI algorithm adaptation in various fields of oil and gas exploration and development, meeting development needs of making the whole chain of upstream business intelligent.

Smart Oil and Gas Exploration Technology   Basin simulation technology, intelligent geophysical exploration and drilling, measuring and well-logging technology, combined with intelligent exploration evaluation and decision-making system, can accurately identify and describe prospect oil and gas reservoirs in real time. Spatial distribution of oil and gas can be accurately predicted, so as to precisely evaluate basin resources in greater details, to conduct science-based and quantitative evaluation of potential and expected reserves. Technical issues: inaccurate samples of massive data, incomplete machine learning leading to ineffective application, being unable to meet needs of smart oil and gas exploration, to fully realize integrated geological fine evaluation and resource prediction.

Smart Oil and Gas Development Technology   Employing colony algorithm, particle swarm optimization (PSO) algorithm and other intelligent algorithm technologies, through digital twins, remote control, ultra-high precision digital modeling technology of ten million grid, and multi-discipline system design, we can do real-time snatching of production dynamic data, factoring reserve utilization rate, recovery rate of oil-gas reservoirs and development benefit and other core indicators into overall consideration, to realize on-line simulation, visual display and dynamic adjustment of wellbore and surface technology, with real-time adjustment and intelligent optimization of development approach. A range of smart technologies for oil and gas reservoirs development is expected to come into being by 2030.

Intelligent Well Formation Technology   This technology adopts genetic algorithm, random forest, artificial neural network and other AI well-forming technologies, to collect all-encompassing data and conduct in-depth data mining, realizing real-time and closed-loop control of ground and downhole equipment, and intelligent decision-making support system for drilling and completion. We need to realize cross-sectoral fusion of traditional drilling and completion of engineering theory and AI technology, achieving comprehensive intelligent drilling guidance, drilling trajectory control, parameter optimization.

（6）Smart Oil and Gas Storage and Transportation

It makes use of industrial big data technology, digital twin and other intelligent technologies, with a large amount of deeply mined data such as detection, monitoring and failure of line and station equipment to build digital twin of storage and transportation system, forming an intelligent technical system that can be monitored and predicted. Technical issues to solve: storage and transportation system that has too many joints and lines, too long distance and wide coverage with highly diversified equipment to present good pipeline equipment running status, plus constraints brought by external environment, making it difficult to come up with accurate judgement regarding resources and market, and to meet the requirements of intelligent management, equipment monitoring, accident forecast and diagnosis of oil and gas storage and transportation system, to eventually realize high efficiency and safe operation of the system.

Intelligent Oil and Gas Pipeline Network Technology Building digital twin of oil and gas pipeline system at various levels can form an intelligent and optimal management system of network operation; in this way holistic and intelligent construction of multi-layer pipeline network can be achieved, which is capable of spherical sensing, comprehensive forecast, adaptive optimization, digital and intelligent overall control of pipeline network system, adaptive to dynamics of external environment and resource market. Technical barriers: digital twin construction of intelligent oil and gas pipeline network, structure and content confirmation of knowledge model, etc. Comprehensive intelligent management, operation, monitoring, prediction and diagnosis of oil and gas pipeline networks will be realized by 2030.

Smart Oil and Gas Storage Technology Through formulation and revision of standards related to digital and intelligent technology of various oil and gas storage systems, intelligent management and technology system of underground storage and tanks is formed, with mapping of virtual production environment to the real one, establishing an intelligent oil and gas storage technology system capable of optimization, prediction and decision-making. Technical barriers to be solved: data availability, complex mechanical model making machine-learning combined into knowledge model difficult; in this way, we can meet the needs of intelligent inventory optimization, intelligent maintenance, intelligent peak adjustment and so on.

Smart LNG Storage and Transportation Technology Digital connection of liquefied natural gas (LNG) receiving, storage, transmission, gasification with gas pipe network, with use of a variety of AI technology, enables construction of an intelligent remote support center of decision-making, which synchronizes production with changes of resource and market, to attain the goal of collaborative optimization of the whole system from receiving, storage, gasification to outward transmission. We should solve the problem concerning integration of whole-process intelligent control technology of LNG system, with storage and transportation theory and AI technology, to realize intelligent control of production process as per demand.

（7）Smart Refining and Chemical Engineering Industry

With construction and application of IT system of refining enterprise as centerpiece, the digital refining and chemical engineering technology applies AI in terms of planning, scheduling, security, environmental protection, energy management, device operation, IT controls, etc., realizing optimization in areas of production and operation, energy management and equipment asset, to reduce cost and improve quality and efficiency.

Intelligent Production Control Integration Technology VR, AR, AI and other technologies are applied to achieve coordinated optimization of the whole industrial chain from raw material transportation and storage to refining and chemical production, oil product storage, to material distribution and other links, so that production and supply can be responsive to market changes. Overall online optimization, based on molecular refining technology, is achieved on refinery production and scheduling. Problems need to be solved: difficulty of achieving optimal allocation between production planning, material supply and market demand; how to make production, control and management, as well as QHSE traceability and monitoring more intelligent so to improve production efficiency, and maximize business performance.

Smart Equipment Safety Monitoring and Control Technology Through self-perception, automatic identification, automatic prediction, adaptive adjustment, failure self-healing and other technologies related to process equipment, the full life cycle intelligent monitoring and control in design, manufacturing, operation, maintenance is realized. Problems to be solved: how to ensure refining and chemical equipments are safe, intelligent and under control, increase carbon clean operation capacity, meet needs of intelligent monitoring and warning, visualized fault diagnosis, web-based monitoring information of equipment, and realize the comprehensive intelligent control of refining and chemical equipment and instruments.

（8）Smart Sales of Oil Products

Based on digital sales technology, oil sales process is smoothed out via application of new technologies such as cloud computing, big data, Internet of Things, mobile communication and AI, improving centralized management of oil product sales data and big data analysis ability, forming a conformant oil retail business management platform and technical system. We should strive to set up standards in the fields of gas station IoT construction and video data collection, generating information gathering ability with all-round perception, to meet the need of in-depth fusion of big data, AI technology and oil sales, promoting customer experience-oriented service innovation, realizing intelligent recognition of license plate, non-inductive pay, digital marketing in convenience stores, so to build a "man, cars and life" multi-business ecosystem.

Online Trading Platform Technology　With the application of block chain, deep learning, etc., to develop insight into customer, industry, market and environment via big data, the service standards of trade unions are established, with the purpose of building service entities with automobile service industry chain as mainstay, consolidating and empowering development of industry chain, expanding eco-system of online service from refueling to car-use, and life service, creating "people, cars and life" ecology, so to promote eco-construction of green energy industrial service.

Smart Gas Station Technology　This technology is centered on gas stations, with online trading platform attracting and guiding customers, realizing on-site intelligent service of oil and non-oil products, with all kinds of refueling service-focused scenarios, based on IoT, AI technology and intelligent terminal, through intelligent broadcast, automatic identification of vehicles, refueling robot, intelligent customer recognition, non-inductive pay, automatic replenishment; in this way, to bring more diversified service to customer with better experience is achieved.

（9）Smart Coal Geo-exploration

The technical system that is defined by multi-dimensional vertical exploration theory and technical measures covering sky, ground surface, well hole, underground, working face, long hole, is to be established; in this way we can make it possible to evaluate coal resources and mining conditions of 1000-meter-deep reserves in an overall and detailed sense, consolidating spatial big data of ground drilling, geophysical, geochemical prospecting and remote sensing and all kinds of underground exploration outcomes, so to conduct in-process dynamic detection and real-time monitoring, early warning of coal mining, meeting the requirements of geological guarantee of unmanned or intelligent mining.

Smart Coal Geology Remote Sensing Technology　It is created on the basis of integration of digital and intelligent data transmission, processing technology, leveraging massive data transmission with low delay of 5G technology, shifting from ex-post processing and distribution to on-orbit real-time transmission of remote sensing image data, to shorten temporal gap between target image capture and information extraction, improving accuracy and timeliness of coal exploration and dynamic monitor of mining.

We need to further solve problems such as low data transmission and processing efficiency, information reception lag, and low precision of processing results of digital coal geological remote sensing technology. This kind of technology can be promoted and applied in coal detection, environmental monitor, geo-disaster monitoring and other fields.

High Speed Wireless Data Transmission Airborne Electromagnetic Technology　This technology makes use of 5G technology in the respect of multi-antenna transceiver and high throughput of big data, turning digital AEM technology from post-detection data processing to real-time data processing, which is more intelligent in advantages such as fast detection, high-speed transmission and real-time monitoring. We need to further solve problems regarding low altitude information network such as data transmission and human-computer interaction, so to provide geological information of deep coal seam in real time, realizing real-time data transmission and processing to proceed with fast detection.

（10）Smart Coal Development

The core factors to focus on the construction of an intelligent coal mine is on mining and production, integrating personnel, equipment and environment, which can realize intelligent fully-mechanized mining and rapid tunneling under different geo conditions; we should also try to achieve intelligent transportation and continuous auxiliary transportation, intelligent power supply and distribution, production safety monitoring, comprehensive management and control and big data analysis, etc.

Full Face Intelligent and Fast Tunneling Technology of Underground Coal Mine　This technology is targeted at oversize mine shaft, slope, fast tunneling and non-blasting construction; research is done on explosion-proof shaft boring machine, shaft drill, full section rock tunnel boring machine and ex-post assembled transportation and bolstering equipment, to come up with design method based mine structure and technical standard system, to develop remote visualized monitoring platform for digging anchor, to meet requirement of 5.0-10.0 meters diameter shaft, slope and tunnel, lifting overall tunneling speed to 200-300 meters/month with 40% reduction of personnel, thus, creating demonstration project of intelligent rapid tunneling of hard rock coal mine

Smart Mining Technology　This technology is to establish and improve information database to meet the needs of intelligent coal mine development, to standardize data verification, data cache, data interface in process of information collection, and to gradually form holographic generalized high-precision intelligent perception field covering whole mine. An open, safe and intelligent coal mine big data sharing and application platform with easy data availability and processing ability will be established to realize seamless access to, as well as deep fusion and processing of data information such as the subsystems, sensors and intelligent devices at deep coal bed, providing data sharing and systemic joint control and support for upper-layer application business modules. The integrated control of all subsystems of smart coal mine rests with real-time, transparent and clear whole-system scene platform covering mining, excavation, machinery, transportation and communication. Technical barriers of the technology to be solved: synchronous transmission of big data, remote real-time control and centralized access of multi-sensors in intelligent mining of coal mines; in this way the efficient data mining and use can be achieved, so to help make intelligent optimized holistic decisions and realize coordinated, highly efficient operation of all systems in intelligent mining of coal.

(11) Low-carbon Transformation of Coal

Large Scale Grading Conversion Technology of Low Grade Coal Key researches of this technology are focused on multi-scale refined separation of raw coal and basic theory of enhancing efficiency and quality, as well as R&D of technology and equipment of large scale grading conversion of low grade coal, so to increase middle distillate products through coal tar total distillate hydrogenation at medium/low temperature, to improve the technology of light fuel making from low/medium temperature coal tar, and other key technologies including hydrogen production from gas without changing concentration, graded utilization and treatment of coal chemical multi-generation wastewater, coal tar hydrogenation exhaust gas recycling, to attain the goal of building 200-ton semi-coke demonstration plant and ten million ton demonstration project of industrialized graded utilization of low grade coal (fat oil dry coal) with pulverized coal pyrolysis.

Coal Liquefaction and High-end Chemical Preparation Technology We need to perfectthe following key technologies and equipment: large scale and efficient gasifier with daily coal feeding capacity of 3000-4000 tons/day and large air separation unit with high efficiency, large methanol synthesis tower, methanation reactor, large scale high pressure compressor, promoting construction of million-ton level and above demonstration project featuring indirect coal liquefaction and high-end chemical products (such as alpha olefin, high-grade lubricate, metallocene polyethylene).

(12) Integrated Energy Technologies

Combined with modeling and simulation, collaborative planning, operation control and maintenance, this kind of technology helps achieving joint production, conversion, multi-form storage and multi-link coordination of various energy sources based on technologies of integration of wind-PV-storage, distributed multi-network power supply and phase change energy storage.

Integrated Technology of Wind-PV-storage With wind power generation, solar power generation, energy storage as major energy facilities, through coordinated operation of multiple facilities, this technology can provide stable and flexible power supply, assisting transmission and absorption of more wind and solar power,as well as improving overall efficiency of power generation system. The technology is mainly applied in the supply side and user side integration of wind-PV-storage, achieving coordinated control and intelligent optimization of wind power, solar power, energy storage system in line with power generation plan, load and output forecast, etc. It can improve accuracy of output curve, smooth out renewable energy output, and improve power quality, etc. We need to further solve the following problems: instability of renewable energy generation and tracking new energy generation schedule; this technology can be applied to scenarios of integrated supply side and demand side with bigger share of renewable energy and integrated wind-PV-storage charging station.

Distributed Multi-generation Technology It provides users with electricity, heat, cold energy, steam, domestic hot water and other energy, through holistic use of natural gas, renewable energy and other clean energy, effectively realizing multi-tiered utilization of energy, with energy comprehensive utilization efficiency reaching 70% -90%. It features distributed supply, clean and pro-environment, highly efficient and independent operation, based modular construction, etc. Problems need to be solved: interconversion of distributed energy, efficient utilization, multi-energy collaborative coupling, etc. Advanced information and communication technology will be used to create digital twin of energy station, making it suitable for regional users that need to access electricity, heat, cold and other energy, etc., such as business centers, schools, hospitals, residential areas and other scenes.

Phase Change Energy Storage Technology It is a new way of high energy storage based on phase-change material(PCM) for energy storage, exploiting theory of phase change where material absorbs or releases latent heat to store energy in the process of changing phase such as solidification/melting, coagulation/gasification, de-sublimation/ sublimation, etc. It can be classified into solid-liquid change, liquid-gas and solid-gas phase change and so on, characterized by constant temperature and higher heat storage density. Problems need to be solved for this technology: intermittent heat supply or mismatch between supply and demand; it can be applied in solar thermal utilization, electric heating, waste heat and residual heat recovery and reuse, energy saving in industrial and residential buildings and air conditioners.

Integrated Energy Modeling and Simulation Technology　Systematic simulation analysis method is used to analyze working mechanism, dynamic characteristics and fault scenarios of integrated energy, including modeling and simulation of integrated energy station and energy transmission network, providing theoretical basis for planning, design and operation of integrated energy system. Given high complexity in parameters such as time, space and behavior, we need to address the following technical issues: integrated energy system dynamics analysis, operation simulation, etc. The technology can be used in design and planning of integrated energy system and operation scheduling, to direct equipment configuration and forecast of operation process based on simulation results, providing necessary means for system planning and scheduling operation.

Integrated Energy Synergetic Planning Technology　On the basis of scientific selection of various distributed energy types and technology routes, this kind of technology can optimize configuration of various energy infrastructure, equipment capacity, system topology, design in big-picture term of business models, meeting users' needs for electricity, heat, cold energy, and gas, to attain the goal of safety, efficiency, economy, and environmental protection. This technology is unique in having multiple input parameters, constraints, optimization objectives, and technical routes. We need to deal with the problem that it is difficult to optimize multi-energy coupling planning and design in an all-round multi-faceted manner, merely depending on single energy planning method. It can be applied to all kinds of integrated energy systems in industry, construction and transportation.

Integrated Energy Operation Control Technology　Based on intelligent sensing, communication, control and intelligent platform technologies, load prediction, modeling and simulation technologies adopted to profile safe and economic operation status of the system, it can strike a balance between supply and demand of electricity, heat, cold and other energy through making adjustment on system by giving operation instructions. Targets of technical control include integrated energy equipment start/stop, output, and connection of all kinds of load of virous amount. Technical barriers are as follows: balance of supply and demand of various energy in an area, balanced distribution on multiple temporal scales or multi-dimension. It is suitable for more complex integrated energy operation scenarios including distributed multiple generation, PV, energy storage and charging infrastructure.

Integrated Energy Operation and Maintenance Technology　This technology works on AI, big data, cloud platform and other technologies, with knowledge graph database stemmed from knowledge and experience of O&M personnel working on site; it can support the development of a series of system tools tailor-made for specific situation, combining UAVs, robots, and other devices to support smart maintenance, inspection, management and other operations of integrated energy system, such as safety assessment, failure diagnosis, intelligent checking, equipment health analysis, etc. The technology is capable of managing multiple types of equipment involved in multiple professions; it is applicable as well under complex operation conditions. Technical barriers are as follows: complex operation of integrated energy, difficulty in optimizing equipment operation, timely and accurate prediction and early warning of faults. It can be applied to industrial parks, buildings and transportation, and other integrated energy consumption scenarios.

Postscript

China has been embarking on a new journey of building a modern socialist country in an all-round way. In the new stage of development, in order to implement new philosophy of development, all industries in China should attach greater importance to innovation-driven, coordinated, green and open development, with a view to promoting people-centered and shared development. In the face of major changes unseen in a century and strategic vision of the rejuvenation of the Chinese nation, digitalization and low-carbon development are the most fundamental and transformative strengths. China's modernization drive requires support of a modern energy system, which is green, low-carbon, smart, efficient, economically secure, and capable of shoring up China's strategic goal of achieving peak carbon dioxide emissions and carbon neutrality by "3060".

Never before in human history has a country taken initiative to strive for carbon peaking with carbon neutrality at its core, when it has yet to complete industrialization and modernization. With neither international experience to draw on nor its own experience to carry forward, China is to encounter formidable challenges without doubt. Therefore, against the big backdrop of digitalization and low-carbon development, to push forward energy technology revolution in China, we need to free ourselves from the tyranny of conventional practice and habitual thinking, making breakthroughs in fields of theory, technology, application and industrial boundaries, to deepen institutional reform on energy and science and technology systems, through overall planning, efficient construction, science-based operation, to empower data, making "object, procedures, rules" in energy industry and enterprises digitalized, promoting development of digital industry and transforming traditional industries with digital technologies. Innovative policy shall be formulated to support science and technology development in the sector, with emphasis on integration of new generation of information and digital technology, and clean efficient exploitation and utilization of energy, blazing a digital trail to advance the revolution of energy technology.

Aiming at in-depth exploration of China's energy technology revolution, *Progress Report on China's Energy Revolution—Energy Technology Revolution (2021)*, elaborates on progress and achievements scored in energy technology revolution in China since 2014, systematically combs through series of technologies and direction of energy technology revolution, which is low-carbon oriented, digital and intelligent development focused. More than 100 scientific problems, already tackled, or to be solved in the future are presented in this book, in hopes of providing valuable references to practices of China's energy technology revolution. We are looking forward to the publication of this Report, hopefully it will stimulate passion from all walks of life to make efforts and share pearls of wisdom in respect to science and technology innovation in energy sector. Now, we would like to express our heartfelt gratitude to relevant departments, research institutes, universities, industrial associations, enterprises, international organizations and many experts for their strong support and great help. Sincerely thanks go to Metallurgical Industry Press for their great support in report collating, English translation, printing and publishing.

Special thanks to the following academicians for their careful guidance and selfless dedication to compilation of the Report:

MA Yongsheng   YU Junchong   MAO Jingwen   DUO Ji   LIU He

JIANG Yi   TANG Guangfu   DU Xiangwan   LI Yang   LI Gensheng

ZOU Caineng   SONG Yonghua   WU Qiang   JIN Zhijun   ZHOU Xiaoxin

HAO Fang   HAO Jiming   HE Kebin   JIA Chengzao   GAO Deli

GUO Xusheng   KANG Hongpu   HAN Yingduo   XIE Heping

We would like to thank the following experts for proposing amendments to the Report:

KANG Chongqing   CHENG Gang   WEI Feng   WANG Kang

XU Jie   MENG Fanda   LV Fa   YANG Hongrun